Praise for Marlo Schalesky

"Whenever I pick up a Marlo Schalesky book, I know I'm headed for an encounter with Eternity. And that as I turn that last page, I will have been changed. And that my heart will be turned more toward Home."

—Tamera Alexander, *USA Today* best-selling author of
Christmas at Carnton and *A Note Yet Unsung*

"Marlo Schalesky's *Reaching for Wonder* is a wonderful remedy for the hurting heart. Told from the perspective of someone who is facing pain and heartache herself, this author's own experiences assure the reader that they're not alone in their pain and struggle. In pulling back the curtain of our humanness, and using well-known stories from the New Testament, she reveals the loving heart of Father God for his children, the side of God we are sometimes too heartbroken to see, the ultimate truth, leading us to reach for Him. A wonderful balm for the hurting soul."

—Melanie Dickerson, author of *The Orphan's Wish* and *The
Noble Servant*

"Marlo Schalesky is a gifted writer with an inspired ability to bring God's Word to life. Each time I read her work, I am both moved and changed. Her *Wonder* books are required reading for anyone who wants to understand the God whose ways are not our ways, and trust Him still."

—Rebecca Price Janney, award-winning author of 20 books,
including *Easton at the Forks*

"Marlo Schalesky's previous books on wonder touched me deeply. Now, in *Reaching for Wonder*, Schalesky explores suffering and the glorious wonder of encountering Jesus Christ in our pain. Using her gift of teaching—bringing Scripture to life through her writing—Schalesky shows us what it means to seek and encounter Jesus when life hurts."

—Ginny L. Yttrup, award-winning author of *Words, Invisible,*
and *Home*

"Marlo's book, *Waiting for Wonder*, touched me at a deep level. She's a talented writer with a gift for getting to the heart and soul of a subject—and a reader. I can unhesitatingly recommend her newest book in this series, *Reaching for Wonder*. You won't want to miss it."

 —Miralee Ferrell, award-winning author of *Runaway Romance*

"Marlo has a gift for reaching the wounded and bringing hope. Having walked the path of suffering, she knows where to find the light and is eager in all ways to share it."

 —Rene Gutteridge, award-winning author of *My Life as a Doormat* and the Boo Series, head writer at the Skit Guys

REACHING

for

WONDER

Encountering Christ
When Life Hurts

MARLO SCHALESKY

ABINGDON PRESS
NASHVILLE

REACHING FOR WONDER
ENCOUNTERING CHRIST WHEN LIFE HURTS

Copyright © 2018 by Abingdon Press

All rights reserved.

Library of Congress Cataloging-in-Publication Data has been requested.

ISBN 978-1-5018-5778-2

18 19 20 21 22 23 24 25 26 27—10 9 8 7 6 5 4 3 2 1
MANUFACTURED IN THE UNITED STATES OF AMERICA

For Bryan

After my skin has been torn apart this way—
then from my flesh I'll see God.

Job 19:26

Contents

Introduction

The Bible gives us a single encounter, a brief moment in time in which a person in pain encountered a Messiah, a Savior. A single instance of what it looks like to see his face in the hardest times of life. A glimpse of a hand reaching, a heart touching, a God who beckons us to see him through our struggle.

I ponder this God for whom simple healing is not enough. He insists on the encounter. He insists I see. When I am afraid to hope, afraid to reach, afraid to pray one more prayer. When I am mute and I am blind. What does it mean to encounter him then?

What does it mean to encounter him in the dark?

I stand beside my son's bed at two in the morning. He lies there, tubes attached, equipment in a pouch around his waist. Blond curls frame his face, shadowed lashes touch his cheeks, illuminated only by starlight.

He sleeps.

I do not.

A breeze sneaks through the window, lifts the curtains. I adjust his blanket, watch for his chest to rise, to fall.

He is alive. For now. But there's no guarantee. Not anymore. Not ever again.

I pull out his blood glucose meter and shove in a test strip. I wait for the beep. Then I take a sleeping boy's finger and make him bleed. Rough fingers, calloused from poke after poke after poke. He does not wake. For him, it has become a familiar suffering.

Dare to encounter the living God, and hope again.

For me, the pain will always be fresh. My son, seven years old, happy, innocent, beautiful, and diabetic. Type 1 diabetes, a disease that could steal his life in a single night, or steal it over years. A cruel disease, and a fickle one.

I hate it. No cure, no cause, no prevention, and no life without the insulin that his own pancreas will no longer provide. I provide it now. If he has enough, he lives. Too much, he dies. It is a delicate dance, every day, every night, every minute, every hour, his life held in the tiny vial of clear liquid attached by tubing through his skin.

So I stand in the darkness and listen to him breathe. I test. I hope. I fight the fear. Will the number be too low? Will it be too high? Will I be monitoring all through the night so that this otherwise healthy boy will greet me in the morning? Will I ever sleep soundly again?

I sigh. I will not cry. Not tonight. Not again. I gather his blood on the tiny test strip. I count to five. Five long seconds that feel like a spin of the roulette wheel. Five eternities because I am no gambler.

And like roulette, there is a number. Seventy-five. Too low. I am not a winner tonight.

I shake him. "Jayden, wake up." He groans but doesn't wake. I pull out a piece of dried fruit strip and shove it into his mouth. He chews, eyes closed. I watch for him to swallow, to make sure he does not choke. Ten seconds. Twenty. His throat moves.

I breathe again. Constant vigilance. Constant concern. The life of my precious son, hanging in the balance of blood sugars.

This is the pain I endure. This is the suffering I cannot escape. Day after day. Night after night. Watching, waiting, hoping and afraid to hope. An incurable disease. A beloved son.

But my pain is not unique. It is no greater, no less than yours. A lost job, a broken marriage, an estranged child, an untimely death, a scary diagnosis, an incurable disease . . . none of us get through the journey on earth unscathed. None of us have life just as we wish it.

We are not who we wanted to be. Sometimes we are a woman who's had five husbands and the man she has now is not her husband. Sometimes we live with shame. Sometimes we are a widow with a dead son. Sometimes we've lost everything we hold dear. Sometimes we're sick, lame, and blind. And sometimes we've been that way so long we don't know how to be well. Sometimes we want to believe, but our faith has failed us. And sometimes, our hurt and hopelessness go so deep that all we can do is walk away.

I've been there. Maybe you have too. Maybe you've stood in the dark and believed life is naught but a spin of the wheel. Maybe you've prayed until you cannot pray anymore. Maybe you've come to a point where all you can see is the pain.

And that's where Christ encounters us.

He encounters us in the heat of the day, on the dusty paths, in the crowds and the dark rooms, on the side of the sea, and on the road out of town when all hope seems lost. In our worst moments, he comes to bring living water, to break the darkness and break the bread. He opens our eyes when we cannot see until all we can see is him.

So I invite you to walk. Walk through these stories of the New Testament's one-time encounters with Christ. See the depth and purposes of a God whose plans and passion go far beyond our healing. They restore our sight. They restore our soul . . . even, and especially, in those moments when life hurts the most.

Come, dare to encounter the living God, and hope again.

If you are willing, you can make me clean.

Mark 1:40 NIV

See also Mark 1:41-45; Matthew 8:1-4; Luke 5:12-16.

1

Reaching Through Doubt

If You Are Willing

*I*f. A tiny word. And yet it holds the world in its hands. *If you want. If you are willing. You can make me clean.* If . . . that single word echoes in my soul, and I know we must start the journey here at *If*. Not *if* you can. Not *if* you have the power. Not even *if* I do it all right. *If* you are willing. *Lord, are you willing to make me whole?*

I look at the question spoken by this man with a skin disease, a disease that ostracized him from his community, that made him an outcast. I gaze at it long and hard and find there a mirror to my own doubts, my own fears.

I know God has the strength.

I know he can do anything.

But is he willing? Does he want to?

That's the question that steals my breath, scratches at my faith.

So with trembling I begin this journey of encounter. I whisper, "Are you willing, Jesus, to heal me too? Even me, even now. Is your love enough?" Is it enough to conquer my "If"?

> *Jesus begins by healing what we do not at first see. He first reaches out to heal the ostracism, the rejection, the source of hopelessness and doubt.*

And the leper's story calls out to me, beckons me closer, whispers of a hope in the storm of doubts, of despair, of disappointments.

I take one step toward the leper. I take a step toward his fear. In his healing, can I find my own? Will I see that the question is not so much if Christ is willing, but if *I* am . . . ?

I imagine it happened something like this:

~ A Leper Tells His Story ~

The crowd moves like the Red Sea moved before my ancestors. Great walls of people pressed against each other to avoid touching me, to prevent even the slightest brush against my flesh. They create a path as dry as the ground in my soul. A path that ought to lead to hope. But I am afraid to hope.

I remember all the promises given to my people after their flight from slavery. I remember that our God is redeemer, rescuer, savior. He is to be my strength and my song. I know all that. But it's hard to believe it. So difficult to believe the promises could be for me.

I am an outcast. I am untouchable. I am . . .

"Unclean." I murmur the word.

I'm supposed to shout it. But I can't. I just can't. So I move forward through the parting waves.

A last chance. A final try. An impossible request. But I have nothing left to lose.

My skin flakes and crumbles. My own body betrays me. It started as a small sore. It grew to swallow my life. I used to have plans; I used to have dreams. Once I believed. I was loved, walked with others. I had confidence in what the future would hold. I had confidence in the God of Israel. I have no such confidence now; I have no such dreams.

But if . . . *if* . . .

My *if* is the only thing I bring.

Perhaps I am a fool.

But I still press through the crowd. I still move toward him. He should shun me. The law says to shun me. And yet I don't turn around. I can't. Not today.

I reach him at last. I kneel before him, my hands at my sides. Hands covered in disease. Face marred.

The words spill from me. Too quick. So unsure.

"*If* you are willing, you have the power to cleanse me." I emphasize the *if*. Because sometimes hope is a terrifying burden.

Then, something strange happens. He stretches out his hand toward me. *Is he? No, he wouldn't, he shouldn't.*

He is. This Rabbi, this holy one, this Jesus, he does the unthinkable.

He touches me.

His fingers brush my face, rest on my open wound. I shiver. His hands are warm, calloused, rough, wondrous. It has been years since I felt the touch of another human being. And now, I tremble. His warmth seeps into me, into my soul.

And I wonder, does he want to cleanse me of more than my disease? What does it mean for a man like this to make me whole?

Then, he speaks. "I am willing. . . . Be clean!" Simple words that change everything.

I feel it leave me: the disease, the heartache, the hopelessness. I am clean. Freed. Healed.

I step back and look at my hands, my arms. They are clear. They are clean, perfect. I touch my cheek and revel at the smooth skin I find there.

I am no longer looking at him, no longer facing him. I am looking at me. And what I see astounds me.

He is speaking again, but I am not listening, not really. I am healed! I must tell my family, my relatives, those who were once my friends. I must tell everyone. I am healed!

"Say nothing to anyone. But go, show yourself to the priest."

Nonsense. Say nothing? How can I say nothing? I came with "if." I leave with everything.

Everything but the one who healed me.

Reaching for Wonder

As I write this chapter, I come from discovering a loved one has made some choices that devastate my soul. A shocking discovery, a painful truth. And I'm reeling, blindsided, grasping for hope as I gasp for air. So many things I know about God. Know, and truly do believe. God takes shame and pain and transforms them to his glory. We need but turn to him. Nothing is beyond his reach. As he changed the cross from a symbol of horror and death to one of grace, hope, and life, so he can transform all things. All things, even this. He is able. I reach for that truth like a drowning man, like a woman whose heart is shattered.

I reach, my fingers trembling. And I find in my grip this tiny word, sharp like a shard of glass. *If.* I, too, am afraid to hope.

If you are willing, Lord.

If you are willing, you can redeem even this for your glory and for the redemption of the one I love.

In this place where I feel untouchable, unclean, where I only have "if," I find that it is not I who reaches for God, it is he who reaches for me.

This is my little, weak faith, this is all I can offer. If.

So, like the leper, I offer my doubt before God in the same breath that I offer my faith.

And then I wait. I wait here with these words on the screen and ponder again the leper's story.

Like him, I do not know if God will make this brokenness whole. But I do know that I need more than promises, more than memorized verses, more than the knowledge of God's power. I need a touch from Christ himself.

So, I watch for what this God of mine will do in the face of desperation mixed with doubt, to a man who is unclean, untouchable. To a man filled with my same doubts, my same fears.

Is God's love enough?

And then it happens. "And [filled with compassion], Jesus reached out his hand, [and] touched him" (v. 41). A variation of this verse says that Jesus is "incensed," but his actions speak much more to compassion than anger, which is why most critical editions of the New Testament say "filled with compassion." Compassion caused Jesus to first heal more than the man's surface disease. Compassion caused Jesus to do the unthinkable.

Jesus touched him.

And he touches me.

What's in a Touch?

I am drawn to this strange dichotomy of "if" paired so closely with the confidence of "you can . . ." or "you are able." In the original Greek, the word used for "you are able" is from the verb *dunamis*, from which we get our word "dynamite." It's a strong word. It means this man has no doubt of Jesus's power. But he does have doubts, not that Jesus can, but that Jesus will.

He doubts God's care. His love.

The law made it clear that people with leprosy, a designation used for a variety of skin diseases, were not to be touched lest the person who touched them would also become unclean. So I wonder, as I think about this man ostracized from society, family, friends because of his disease, if the pain, the discomfort, of his disease is actually the lesser thing. I wonder if his leprosy has taken more than his health, if it's taken his heart, his faith, his connection to people who make him feel human.

The isolation, the loneliness, the rejection has become his reality. "If" is born in the barrenness of being alone. In our pain, our hurt, our desperation, it is easier to believe in power than it is to believe in love. It's easier to doubt than to hold hope in trembling hands.

We hear that doubt, that desperation in the leper's silent question: "Jesus, are you willing?"

And Jesus answers. But he doesn't answer the question first. If we rush through this section, we miss the importance of the order of Jesus's actions. Before he says he is willing, he reaches out and touches the man.

He touches the untouchable. He breaks the isolation. He addresses the deepest need, the need for connection to become whole.

We expect Jesus to heal the man of leprosy. But Jesus begins by healing what we do not at first see. He first reaches out to heal the ostracism, the rejection, the source of hopelessness and doubt.

Jesus makes the man whole, not just well, but whole. And he does it by touching him, by reaching, by encountering the man just as he is.

That's how it is with us.

In this place where I feel untouchable, unclean, where I only have "if," I find that it is not I who reaches for God, it is he who reaches for me.

He reaches for me when I cannot.

And suddenly, I dare to hope.

I Am Willing

And in the face of doubt and fear, Jesus speaks not a condemnation, but instead two simple words (in the Greek) that dispel both doubt and fear. The first is, when translated, "I am willing." And the second is, "Be cleansed."

When we are at our lowest, when faith fails, when it hurts to try to hope anymore, God's answer to us is not disappointment or guilt or shame. His answer is, "I am willing." He is willing to make us whole. He loves us enough not just to heal but to make clean.

I discover this God who is willing to give me what I truly need to become all he created me to be.

I love the deeper meaning of the word "to cleanse" in the Greek. It not only means to cure a person from an "unclean" disease, but it also means to free from faults, to free from the doubt we see in "if." It means to consecrate, to dedicate, to make complete for God's use.

That is what Jesus intends to offer us. Not simply a cure for the external need, but a deep soul cleansing that takes our "if" and transforms it into wonder.

He is willing. The question is, are we?

Are You Willing?

The leper was not. He was willing to accept healing, but he left health behind. He would not accept the full meaning of cleansing that Jesus offered. After Jesus healed the man of leprosy, Jesus said,

"Don't say anything to anyone. Instead, go and show yourself to the priest and offer the sacrifice for your cleansing that Moses commanded" (v. 44).

This may look like a command. I see it as a call, an invitation to more, to be consecrated and set aside for God's use. It's an invitation to become not just healed, but a part of something great and beautiful and wondrous. To become a part of Jesus's movement in the kingdom of God.

But the man is not willing. Mark 1:45a tells us, "Instead, he went out and started talking freely and spreading the news so that Jesus wasn't able to enter a town openly."

Instead. I shudder at the word. And my heart breaks.

Because in the face of the great "if," Jesus offered so much more than healing. He offered himself. And yet this man was unwilling to claim the greatest gift of all.

As I consider this disturbing truth, I think about the little, once-wild donkey we recently rescued and brought to Wonder Wood Ranch. She was so thin, ragged, and terrified.

For the first two weeks, she was too afraid to come to the barn and eat. Every day I would haul an armload of hay out to the pasture for her. I could see the "if" in her eyes. She would stand and watch me; sometimes she would let me pet her. Sometimes she wouldn't. She knew I was able to feed her, help her, bring her what she needed to heal. But she didn't know if I was willing to give her more. She didn't know if I cared, if I loved.

I was willing. I am willing.

I fed her, gave her supplements, wormed her, had the farrier out to fix her feet and the vet out to vaccinate. I petted her, brushed her, cleaned her hooves, built a shelter to protect her from the rains.

And the once skinny, bedraggled donkey is now happy, healthy, and able to eat from her feeder at the barn.

But I want more. I want more for her than just physical health. I envision a donkey who finds her joy, her purpose, in bringing hope and healing to disadvantaged kids at Wonder Wood Ranch. I want her to become all that she can be, to fulfill her potential and purpose and leave all her fears behind. I want to take her "if" and bring not only healing but also wholeness.

Jenny may look to me to solve her external problems of hunger and hoof-ache, but I am offering her a chance to be a part of our family, to know love and have a mission and discover the joy of being a part of something wondrous.

In my pain, in my "if," that is what Jesus is offering me too, just as he offered the leper.

God is offering more than healing. He wants to do more than make it better. He is calling us to a mission of love.

He is calling us to show, not tell.

Show, Don't Tell

In the writing world, there's a little phrase that you learn early regarding effective writing. "Show, don't tell," the experts say. Jesus asked the leper to do the same. In Mark 1:44 Jesus instructs the man to "show yourself to the priest. . . . This will be a testimony to them." He calls the man to show what God has done. But instead we read, "He went out and started talking freely" (v. 45). The man didn't show, he told, and in disobeying Jesus, the power of his testimony was lost. We learn that because of this "Jesus wasn't able to enter a town openly."

Despite his healing, the leper got it all wrong. Healing didn't make him obedient. Sometimes in our pain and desperation we think if only God would do this thing we want, then we would respond with faithfulness and submission. The leper tells us . . . maybe not.

It is our short-sightedness that keeps us from all God is willing to do. We look at the hay in the hand and fail to see the one who holds the hay. We fail to see the fullness of what God is offering.

In our pain and desperation, it is not our doubts that keep us from wholeness; we need only come to him with our doubts. "Ifs" in hand, we must simply encounter him, for he is willing to give not just the hay. He is offering himself.

Who Is This God?

Who is this God who hears my doubt and offers not condemnation but more than I can even dream? I mull over that question as I drive away from the home of my friend with ALS. *If you were willing, Lord, you could heal her.*

But he doesn't.

Or does he?

Her ALS progresses. Today she was surrounded with tubes to help her breathe and to pull the mucus from her lungs. Another machine pounded her chest to break up the mucus for removal.

She was able to speak only through the movement of her eyes on a computer screen. She asked how she could pray for me.

I read to her from a book called *Heaven*.

And my soul was filled.

If you are willing, Lord . . .

I am willing.

And in that moment as I approach a stop sign, my mind still caught in the room where my friend sits in her wheelchair amidst the menagerie of machines, I know it's true. God has taken my "if" and transformed it to wonder.

That is the God we have. The God who embraces our "if" and changes it to glory.

He is willing, not to cure the body (at least in this life) but to make my friend whole, and in doing so, to touch me, make me whole, as well. With every labored breath, I see God with her, offering more than physical healing, offering himself—a close, intimate walk through her last stages of life, with him. I see the wonder of a God who can use even this awful ALS as "a testimony to them" (v. 44b) and to me.

People ask me why I go visit my friend when she can no longer speak more than a few computer-generated words, can barely even breathe. They think I am being kind, they think I am faithful. They don't know the truth. I go because there, in the eyes of my friend, I see the God who takes my "if" and makes me whole. I encounter the God who is reaching for me.

And I discover anew that my doubts are no barrier to God's gift of his presence. I discover this God who is willing to give me what I truly need to become all he created me to be.

I find the God of Gideon, who doubted that God was truly calling him to rescue the Israelites from Midianite oppression. Three times in Judges 6 Gideon brought to God his "if" and asked for a sign.

> But Gideon replied to him, "With all due respect, my Lord, if the LORD is with us, why has all this happened to us?" (v. 13)

19

Then Gideon said to him, "If I've gained your approval, please show me a sign that it's really you speaking with me." (v. 17)

But then Gideon said to God, "To see if you really intend to rescue Israel through me as you have declared, I'm now putting a wool fleece on the threshing floor." (vv. 36-37)

Gideon doubted. God encountered. God led. And Gideon received more than a blessing; he received a purpose and the presence of God in it.

That is the God we have. The God who embraces our "if" and changes it to glory.

God is willing, not because of our perfect faith, but despite our stumblings. He loves you. And that is enough.

So come, sit with me and with Gideon, waiting, breath held, our hearts whispering, *Lord, if you are willing . . . so am I.*

*Meet me here, Lord, in my doubts, in my desperation,
in the "if" places of my life. Encounter me, and make me whole.*

Come and see a man who has told me everything I've done!

John 4:29

See also John 4:4-42.

2

REACHING THROUGH SHAME

You've Had Five Husbands

It is what it is. I've said the phrase many times, but never with hope. Never with joy. It is an expression of deep resignation. Sometimes, it's a saying that secretly breaks my heart.

Does it always have to be this way? Is it really too late? Is the life I have all that life will ever become? Are my pain and my shame iron bars of a prison cell? Or perhaps, in the hands of the Messiah, might they be the keys to escape?

I bring my helplessness, my hopelessness, to the well with the Samaritan woman. I search for a thirsty man sitting by its side. I come with bucket empty and heart not daring to hope. But I come. I listen.

I encounter Christ in the story of another woman whose heart beat like mine, whose doubts and fears and shame had made her believe that life could never be anything more.

And I wonder . . . will this stranger by Jacob's well free me too? Will he see me for who I truly am and still make me whole? Can my life be more than *it is what it is*?

Perhaps it happened like this:

⟶ A Samaritan Tells Her Story ⟶

I hate this life. I hate what I am. I hate this dusty path that leads to a well dug by my ancestor. Dug by Jacob himself. He was a deceiver, but God chose him anyway. I am much worse. So shamed, so pained, that I trudge to the well in the heat of the day with the sun beating on my brow and the jar rough in my hands. The jar is empty. It seems always to be empty.

And so the dust swirls, my feet plod, my fingers grip the emptiness.

I hear voices, male and Jewish. I glance up.

A small gaggle of men amble toward me. One drops coins into the money bag of another. "He said to buy food," says one.

"Don't know why he didn't come with us," spouts another.

"Who knows why he does what he does."

They talk on. And I don't care. I cross to the other side of the road, averting my face as if by doing so they will not see me. I am invisible. No one sees me. They never do.

I continue to the well alone, happy to be alone. Unhappy. But what choice is there? The other women come to the well in the cool of the morning. They laugh and gossip and share stories of lives I don't understand. I come now when the sun is at its zenith. I come alone. I draw water alone. I leave alone. Except for the company of my shame.

But not today.

Someone sits at the edge of the well. A man. A mystery. He looks at me and I tremble. Why is there a Jew at the well in the heat of the day? Should I turn back? Should I flee? I need water.

I sigh. I need more than water.

I avert my gaze and sidle to the far side of the well. I am invisible. He will not see me.

A voice shatters the silence. "Give me some water to drink."

I swallow, and for a moment, the whole world stills. Slowly, I lift my eyes to him. He sees me. And I am stunned. Words sputter from my lips. "Why do you, a Jewish man, ask for something to drink from me, a Samaritan woman?"

Does he smile? What is that slight quirk of his lips? That crinkle at the sides of his eyes? "If you recognized God's gift and who is saying to you, 'Give me some water to drink,' you would be asking him and he would give you living water."

Living water? Running water? He makes no sense. He speaks in riddles. But he speaks. To me. And that is something I cannot ignore. "Sir, you don't have a bucket and the well is deep. Where would you get this living water? You aren't greater than our father Jacob, are you? He gave this well to us, and he drank from it himself, as did his sons and his livestock."

His gaze turns thoughtful now, as if he's willing me to hear more than I can hear, see more than I can see. "Everyone who drinks this water will be thirsty again, but whoever drinks from the water that I will give will never be thirsty again. The water that I give will become in those who drink it a spring of water that bubbles up into eternal life."

More riddles. And yet . . . yet . . . If only he knew the truth . . . "Sir, give me this water, so that I will never be thirsty and will never need to come here to draw water!" For a single second, for the slightest breath, I envision what it would be like to be freed from my daily trek of shame. To avoid the whispers that still persist. To hide. From sun and dust and humiliation.

To hide. But I don't imagine what it would be like to be free. I cannot imagine that.

Then he speaks again, his words dropping like boulders into my soul. "Go, get your husband, and come back here." My husband, he says. His face is impassive now. His eyes keen. They watch me. They see too much. I cannot lie. I cannot hide. I should have known I can never hide, even at Jacob's well in the hottest part of the day.

"I don't have a husband." There, I have said it. Not a confession really, but the truth. The smallest bit of truth I can manage. I turn my head, willing him to silence. Desperate that he speak no more. *Please, no more.*

Too late. "You are right to say, 'I don't have a husband. You've had five husbands, and the man you are with now isn't your husband. You've spoken the truth."

And there it is. All my pain, all my shame, my hopelessness, my helplessness. Exposed. Laid bare before this stranger at the well. Five. Six, really. The number that defines everything that has gone wrong, that always goes wrong. This is my life, defined by a number twice what the rabbis allow. And the way he speaks it. He doesn't sneer. He doesn't accuse. He simply says it.

It is what it is. We both know it.

And I believe it's all I will ever be. I cannot speak of this. I must not. Surely there is a safer topic, an old argument between Samaritans and Jews. Let us speak of that. It's easier. Safer. "Sir, I see that you are a prophet. Our ancestors worshiped on this mountain, but you and your people say that it is necessary to worship in Jerusalem."

He answers me with more riddles. He speaks of the Messiah. He speaks of worship in spirit and in truth. Truth. Somehow this man reeks of it. And I can speak nothing else when I am with him. "I know that the Messiah is coming, the one who is called the Christ. When he comes, he will teach everything to us."

"I Am—the one who speaks with you."

His words bridge the gap between us, though neither of us move. I tremble. He has said more than I ever dreamed possible. More than I ever hoped could be true.

I Am.

He is.

Could it be?

What if . . . what if there really is hope in my shame? What if this man, this mystery, really is my Messiah?

And what if that truth is the only thing that matters?

I hear the voices of the Jewish men I passed on the road. They approach but say nothing to their companion at the well. I glance down at the jar that I clutch in my hands. It is empty. I am not.

Living water. I am beginning to understand. I am beginning to believe.

I leave my jar at the well and hurry toward town.

I will tell them everything. I will tell them I met the Messiah. I will tell them we can all be set free.

No.

I cannot tell them that. They must discover it, discover him, as I have.

Instead I will tell them what only I can say. I will speak of the thing that I have always most wanted to hide. I, who snuck to the well at midday to avoid the uncovering of my shame. I, who have had five husbands and the one I have now is no husband at all. I, who carry with me nothing but guilt and an empty clay jug. I am no longer afraid of what they'll say. I am no longer afraid of the shame that has been all I've known.

I will face it. I will face them. I will say, "Come and see a man who has told me everything I've done! Could this man be the Christ?"

And in doing so, I will leave more than just an empty water jar by the well.

Reaching for Wonder

Jesus opens with a question that is an invitation to overcome shame. "Will you give me a drink?" he asks. Or, more directly, "Give me some water to drink." It is an invitation to all of us to choose to draw near or choose to draw back. The Samaritan woman has come at noon to avoid meeting people, she has come to hide in the brightest part of the day.

And Jesus begins with this simple request. To her, to us. Will we give him a chance? Will we engage? Will we take that one step closer as we clutch our empty water jar to our chests?

She could have said no. We can too.

But then we would miss the shocking side of wonder.

The commentaries are long and detailed about this story in John. They speak in depth about the meaning of living water, about worshiping in spirit and in truth, and the implications of being a Samaritan in a Jewish world. There are pages filled with the surprise of Jesus speaking to this woman at a well. Notes and exegesis, suppositions and historical facts. And yet, when I sit with this story of a woman who had five husbands and the man she had now was not even her husband, when I watch her walking to a well at midday, alone, ashamed, solitary, when I envision the slump of her shoulders, the shuffling of her feet, none of the lofty theology or the images of running water are what shake me to my core. What shakes me, disturbs me, shatters my paradigms is not water or worship, it's the words she speaks to her fellow townspeople after she has encountered the living God. "Come and see a man who has told me everything I've done!" (v. 29).

She doesn't say, "Let me tell you about living water." There's not a mention of worship, not even a declaration of new theological knowledge. She speaks just this simple sentence that draws attention

29

to the very shame she had previously gone to great lengths to avoid. She points to her deepest pain, her deepest shame, and uses that to draw others to Jesus.

In our deepest shame and pain, our Messiah is asking us to see the gift of God where we least expect it, to know who is sitting at the well offering us living water in the deepest places of our pain.

What a shocking transformation! Why does it happen? How can this be? And what does this mean for my own pain, for the shame I try to keep most hidden? What does it mean for those times I feel like I'm at the worst of my worst and I'm sneaking to the well at noon? When I'm trying to hide, avoid, because it just can't get any worse and my life's a mess and it's my fault?

This changes everything.

What a Mess!

Maybe we've gotten this story all wrong. Maybe it's not about the transformation of worship or water. Maybe it's about the amazing transformation of a woman, and of us all.

This woman is a Samaritan. The animosity between Jews and Samaritans was well known, dating back to 2 Kings 17 when Assyria conquered the ten northern tribes of Israel and created a mixed race. Jews of the remaining southern kingdom scorned the impure race of the Samaritans.

This woman also experienced dishonor simply for being a woman. Two Jewish rabbinic rules of the day stated, "One should not talk with a woman on the street, not even with his own wife" and "It is forbidden to give a woman any greeting."[1]

But she wasn't just any Samaritan. She wasn't just any woman. She was a woman who'd had five husbands when the rabbis had declared that three was the maximum for decency. And worse yet, she was having sexual relations with a man who didn't even value her enough to marry her.

A Samaritan. A woman. And a life steeped in immorality and sin. Her life was a mess. Broken dreams, broken relationships, a broken spirit. This was not the life she had hoped for. This was not the life she planned for when she was a little girl. But this is the life she carried with her when she brought her water jar to the well.

Her shame is palpable as we envision the heat of the sun at midday, a time when no one else would come to the well. Other women came in the morning to draw water for the day, chat, and be a community with one another. But she has no community. She has no husband. We hear no mention of sons to care for her. She has no respect, no support, no hope for a life better than the one she has. That hope died at least three men ago. For her, life has gone from bad to worse, to worse yet. And that shame has become the center of who she is.

Scholar D. A. Carson says, "Now, relating the steps in her thinking to her people, she exhorts them, Come, see a man who told me everything I ever did—which may be hyperbole, but quietly attests how central her messy and sinful personal life was to her own thinking."[2]

Our own mess is often central to our thinking as well. We view our lives and we view Christ through the lens of our shame.

We hide, we divert attention from our faults, we go to the well at noon because we're focused on our mess and we think it's all everyone else sees. Our souls long for living water, but we cannot receive it until we empty the jar of our shame and stand before Jesus with our masks discarded and our jars no longer clutched to our chests.

The Transformation of Shame

The Samaritan woman came to Jesus with nothing but that jar and her mask of shame. Jesus began by asking her to give him a drink. The request seems simple enough. After all, he was tired and thirsty and didn't have a container to draw water. But it isn't simple at all.

Because in asking for a drink, Jesus was also asking her to choose to encounter him instead of clinging to her identities of disgrace. Everything about her, her race, her gender, her social status, her sin, should have separated her from the Jewish Messiah-man at the well. But in his simple request for water, Jesus invited her to lay all that aside and approach him.

He asks the same of us.

And then, he asks more.

He asked her, as he asks us, to engage with him. "If you recognized God's gift . . . you would be asking him," he says to the woman. In our deepest shame and pain, our Messiah is asking us to see the gift of God where we least expect it, to know who is sitting at the well offering us living water in the deepest places of our pain. He calls us to ask for more than just to serve him, more than to cover up our sin, more than putting a little water in our jars and saying, "This is what I'm giving to God." He says to us, "Understand who I am and the amazing grace I offer you, even, and especially, when you least deserve it."

The woman offered objections. So do we. "You don't have a bucket," she said. Do we also believe that Jesus doesn't have what he needs to give us what we need? Does it seem impossible? Does the well of shame seem too deep?

Despite our doubts, in the face of them, Jesus offers us "a spring of water that bubbles up into eternal life" (v. 14).

"Give me this water," the woman said.

But Jesus couldn't give it yet. Instead, he had to uncover the real reason she could not yet receive. "Go, get your husband."

She replied, "I don't have a husband." She tells the truth, a small truth, but a truth all the same.

And it is enough of a confession for Jesus to blow the lid off her shame. "You've had five husbands, and the man you are with now isn't your husband."

The truth. Bold, unhidden, and now fully uncovered. Not condemning, not angry, just "it is what it is." No more hiding, no excuses, and because of that, a new, surprising hope: *It is what it is, but it's not the way it always must be.*

She was resigned to her shame. He was not.

As writer and singer Michael Card says, "As gently as a doctor unwraps a wound to examine it, Jesus takes the cover off her life. The wounds are deep: there were five slashes of woundedness, and even now there is an ongoing injury because she lives with a man whose love cannot embrace her as his wife. She is discovered—uncovered."[3]

Even when she deflects the conversation with questions of theology, Jesus continues to engage with her. The truth is out, her heart is open.

And to heal her, Jesus does not go around her shame, he goes through it.

In our own places of hiddenness and guilt, Jesus will not allow us to cover up, dress up, play down our shame or our pain. He doesn't want to minimize it, he wants to transform it. He wants to pull away our veils, our excuses, our attempts to divert his gaze from the truth . . . and make us new.

Just as he made the Samaritan woman new. And he did so not through the promises of living water, not through the theology of worship or the mystery of a Messiah. It is the straight, unadorned truth that truly broke through this woman's pain. Ugly, painful, hurtful, and the very key to set her free from her prison of shame. Jesus says in John 8:32, "Then you will know the truth, and the truth will set you free." He speaks regarding not just the truth about him and his identity but also the raw truth about herself.

We know this because when the disciples arrived back at the well, the woman left her jar, left her emptiness and shame behind her, and went directly to the townspeople whom she had previously tried to avoid. Her words give an amazing insight into the transformation of her shame. She told them to come see a man who uncovered her shame, called it what it was, and made her not ashamed of it anymore. She led with the very thing she most wanted to hide. And verse 39 says they believed because of her word when she testified. And what is her testimony? Not that she's found the Messiah. Not that she's discovered living water. Not even the truth about the theological debates of her day. Her testimony is not her knowledge, but the transformation of her shame.

That's the power of the truth spoken by Jesus into our lives. The power to transform our deepest shame into our greatest tool for his glory, for drawing others to him. She spoke only the tiniest truth, "I have no husband." But spoken to Jesus, it was enough to help her face the whole truth, and instead of destroying her, it set her free.

So why are we so afraid of the truth? Why do we so want to hide? When my children were little, they would put a hand over their eyes and believe that I somehow couldn't see them. I have a horse who will hide his face in the corner of his pen and think that he has been rendered invisible. The truth is, we're all like that, especially if we've done something we're ashamed of. We cover up, we hide, and we think somehow we can't be seen.

But God sees. God knows. And instead of condemning he wants to restore. He wants to give us the gift of *aletheia*. In New Testament Greek, *aletheia* is the word for truth, but it comes from a root word meaning unhidden. So when Jesus says, "the truth will set you free," he means that this freedom he offers includes this gift of grace: We don't have to hide anymore. We don't have to be ashamed.

Too often we think we bring others to Christ by how much we know. But this encounter with Jesus by a shamed Samaritan woman at Jacob's well tells us that *aletheia* is what calls people to "come and see." It's the unhiddenness, the truth, of who we really are. All the scars, all the mistakes, all the mess . . . we need not point to Jesus around it, we must point through it. Because there, like a mosaic of broken glass, we find that Jesus has taken our shards and made them into something beautiful. He has made his light to shine through in beauty and amazing wonder.

The Empty Jar

So I consider my own life-jar, clutched to my chest, filled with shame and pain. I think about how I come to the well in the heat of the day and believe no one will see as I try to fill my need with water than only runs dry and never quenches the true thirst of my soul.

And then I consider a Samaritan woman who dropped her jar completely because she didn't need it anymore. She had encountered the living God, and her shame had been transformed into the very thing she used to draw others to this Messiah. It was not about her anymore; it was about him.

Commentator Paul Louis Metzger observes, "She no longer cares what they think of her because she knows that the Messiah is near and that he cares for her. Jesus redeems her story. She is no longer ashamed of it."[4]

That's what Jesus wants to do for me too. And for you. But we must go to the well, bringing him the empty water jar. We must engage. We must encounter the living God in the form of the Messiah.

We must discover this God of the empty jar.

Who Is This God?

There's something about empty jars at Jesus's feet: the Samaritan woman by the well, the woman who wept and dried Jesus's feet with her hair in Luke 7. In that passage of Luke, we read about a sinful woman who brought an alabaster jar of perfumed oil to the house of a Pharisee and, after crying and wiping Jesus's feet, she kissed them and poured out the perfume from her jar. She emptied her jar. "I tell you that her many sins have been forgiven," Jesus said in response (Luke 7:47). She came with her sorrow and her sins and she left her jar at his feet. She left forgiven and filled with new hope.

There is something about leaving our emptiness with him. Something about leaving all our shame, guilt, ugliness of the past . . .

and walking away new. And that's what it means to drink of the living water. That's what it means to worship in spirit and in truth. We pour out our jar of perfume at his feet and worship him. We drop our jar, and our shame, and worship him with the words, "Come and see a man who has told me everything I've done!"

Our God is the God of the Empty Jar.

We must only bring our hidden shame, our hidden pain, our emptiness.

Jesus is waiting for you, for me, at the edge of the well in the heat of the day. Will you bring your jar to him?

> *Lord, help me to trust you enough to come to the well*
> *and leave my empty jar at your feet.*
> *Uncover my shame and transform it for your glory.*

They couldn't carry him through the crowd, so they tore off part of the roof above where Jesus was. . . . When Jesus saw their faith, he said to the paralytic, "Child, your sins are forgiven!"

Mark 2:4-5

SEE ALSO MARK 2:1-12; MATTHEW 9:1-7; LUKE 5:17-26.

3

REACHING THROUGH HELPLESSNESS

Lowered Through a Roof

I've always loved this story of faithful friends tearing a hole in the roof of what was probably Peter's house. I love their faith and their daring. I love the images of dirt and clumps of dried mud falling around Jesus. I love to imagine him looking up and smiling at the faith of those friends.

But what about the paralyzed man? What could he see, what did he experience? Jesus never mentioned his faith. And why did Jesus offer forgiveness before physical healing?

Who is this Jesus who forgives and heals when I can't do anything but lie on my mat?

I ponder these questions and find myself looking into the eyes of a man on a mat and seeing myself reflected there. What does it mean to come to Jesus in utter helplessness? How does the paralyzed man's encounter with Jesus speak to the places in my life where there's nothing I can do, when I don't have the faith to be made whole? Who is this Jesus who forgives and heals when I can't do anything but lie on my mat?

Perhaps it happened something like this:

A Paralyzed Man Tells His Story

I've lived in Capernaum my whole life. I grew up here, learned to walk, learned to fish. Learned how to make nets and clean them. How to barter and watch for storms stirring on the horizon of the Sea of Galilee. But I never learned how to live without the sway of the sea beneath my feet, the smell of waves in my nostrils, the rough texture of the nets in my hands. There is nothing beneath my feet now. And I cannot feel with my hands. I've lived in Capernaum all my life. I died here too.

At least I wish I had. Instead I live this breathing death. The death-life of a paralytic. I will never learn how to live like this.

I remember so well the flex of my muscles as we pulled in a load of fish. The fierce grip of my fingers on the mast. The gentle clasp of a child's hand in my own. I could carry a friend's son on my shoulders. I could carry the world.

Now, I cannot even carry my mat. I can't get myself from my bed to the corner of the street outside to beg for bread. I can't eat without help, or dress, or relieve myself. Or find the will to find peace.

How could the God of Israel let this happen to me? What sin have I committed?

I stop there. For a moment, I hold my breath.

I know too well my sins, my failings, the thoughts that eat holes in my mind.

I am not a faithful man. I am not noble. I am not brave. I am struggling, sad, bitter. I would take death if I could. But I can't even accomplish that. I am helpless, hopeless. Paralyzed, not just in my body, but in my soul.

If there is a God in Israel, he has forgotten me.

But my friends have not.

They bustle now through the door, hurry toward my bed. Four of them. Five. More. I only need two to take me to the street corner. They see my confusion.

Joses laughs. "We're not taking you to the street corner today, my friend. The healer has come." He glances toward the others. "We have bigger plans."

The healer? Jesus, Joseph's son? I have heard of him. Prophet. Rabbi. And whispers of how he heals. He heals people like me.

"He's at Simon's house, the one they now call Peter."

Cephas, the Rock. Simon is a rock as much as I am a runner. But I listen anyway as my friends babble on about this Jesus and their plans for me. Snippets about a dove descending on this carpenter's son, about baptism in the Jordan River, about driving out evil spirits and a doubting man healed of leprosy.

They are especially excited about that one.

Simeon shakes my shoulder. "He heals from leprosy. He'll heal you too. Just imagine . . ."

But I can't imagine.

Then the others join in. "We just need to get you to Jesus." "It's crowded at Peter's house." "Can we get the mat through?" "We could carry it." "Surely people will get out of the way."

And then the voice of my closest friend, "Even if they don't, we'll find a way. We have to find a way."

They're so sure, so confident in this Jesus. Don't they know I'm beyond healing? Beyond hope. Helpless. I think I hate that most of all. The helplessness. The despair. The sickening knowledge that there is nothing I can do to make this right. There is nothing I can do but lie on my bed and allow them their faith.

They are so full of faith.

I am just full of a dead kind of fear.

Two grab my shoulders, another my legs. Two more bring the mat. I want to object, but I say nothing. The words in my throat are as paralyzed as I am.

So they heave me onto the mat. Four of them grab it up, with me on it, and the others follow. Joses and Matthias, Jeremiah and Eliakim, Joram and Simeon and Eliud. We've been friends since we were boys. And though I told them to leave me when I was paralyzed, they would not.

They still won't.

They heft me up, through the door, out into the street. I can't see the street, only the sky, bright blue above me. A few wisps of clouds. I hear the pattering of many feet. We move slowly. Carrying me slows them down.

They will not be able to hear Jesus speak. Everyone else will get there first.

I am a burden and not a friend. Why won't they just leave me behind?

As if he can hear my doubts, Matthias leans toward me. "Tomorrow you'll cast nets again with us. You'll feel the sway of the sea beneath your feet. The healer will make it so."

I have heard he heals bodies, but can he heal hearts? I dare not speak the words aloud.

I focus on the sound of thudding feet all around me. Groups hurry past. They murmur about the rabbi coming home, about the Pharisees who already took the best places to hear him. Pharisees. I wonder if Nashon is one of them. He was the first to tell me I deserved my paralysis because of my sin. He was the first to explain that God had cursed me, and I was to blame. He may be right. But didn't David sing of God forgiving sins?

The footsteps rush ahead and fade until only the patter of my companions disturbs the dust. And still we plod on toward Simon's house. In time, I hear the sound of feet again, this time shuffling, no footsteps. I hear the rustle of bodies and breathing. No one speaks.

We push forward. I turn my head and see the crowd. We have arrived at Simon's house. Vaguely, I hear a voice from inside. The voice of the one they call Jesus. But it is far away and the sound of the crowd outside the door blurs his words. We press on. The crowd squeezes in. It will not part. We try another spot. No one gives way before us.

Matthias points to his left. "Look."

I strain my neck but cannot tell what they see. All I see is sky. And crowds bunching on the horizon.

I should have known this would never work.

My mat moves sideways. Around the crowd. And then, I

am ascending. Jostling. Bumping. Bustling. I almost fall off. I cannot steady myself.

I hate the helplessness.

But my friends continue to drag me upward.

And suddenly, I am lying on my mat on the roof. They are kneeling, arms pulling at something I can't see. But I can hear the sounds. Crunching, ripping, exclamations from people below. And I can smell the dirt, the pungent aroma of old mud exposed and broken. Bits of it float up, glint in the sunlight.

Bits of dirt and old mud. They settle in my soul. They are not the only filth I carry there.

My friends stand. What are they doing? They couldn't be. They can't.

They are.

I am descending now. All I can see is their faces, sweat dripping, eyes shining through the hole they've made in Peter's roof.

They believe.

Eliud smiles. I do not smile back. I am terrified and angry and afraid and . . .

Eliud's glance slips away, settles on something below me. His countenance changes. It's almost like his face reflects a glory I cannot yet see.

And for a moment I have hope. Ridiculous, stupid, crazy hope.

I bump into the floor. Short ropes loosen and fall. Faces are still above me, but I don't see them. I don't see anything. Not my friends, not the sun shining through the hole in the roof, not the crowd or the Pharisees.

All I see is him. This one who looks down at me with eyes that look not at me but into me. And I know he sees. He sees not just the palsy without but the paralysis within. He sees the sin that no paralysis can hide.

He speaks. Loud enough for the crowd, the Pharisees, to hear. Quiet enough to shatter my soul. "*Teknon.*" He calls me son, child. I'm a grown man, but he sees the frightened boy in the shell of a body. If there is a God in Israel . . .

I am not forgotten after all.

"Your sins are forgiven."

He sees, he knows, he forgives. He heals the deeper need. If I could, I would weep. But I do not. I cannot.

Murmuring skitters through the crowd. And then he is looking not at me but away. His face hardens. I do not move my gaze from him. I wait . . .

"Why are you questioning these things in your hearts?"

Who is he speaking to? Not to me. I have no questions. Not now. My sins are forgiven. Somehow, I have no question about that.

"Which is easier—to say to a paralyzed person, 'Your sins are forgiven,' or to say, 'Stand, pick up your mat, and walk'?" (Matthew 9:5).

Now I know. He speaks to the Pharisees. He speaks on my behalf. There is a God in Israel.

But there is no answer to his question. Not from the Pharisees, not from the crowd. Not even from me. Because we know both are impossible: for a man to forgive sins and for a paralytic to be healed. This Jesus has done the first impossibility. Will he heal my body as well?

"But so that you may know that the Son of Man has authority to forgive sins on earth . . ." His gaze rests on me again. It is fierce. It is gentle. It is love. "Stand, pick up your mat, and go home." He reaches for me. His hand grasps mine. And he lifts me.

And I feel the world under my feet. My legs strong. My back straight. My arms tingling.

I lean over and pick up my mat in sturdy hands. My fingers respond to my thoughts. My shoulders square.

The crowd parts, and I walk out in front of them all.

I hear them whisper, "We've never seen anything like this."

But he has done more than they can see, he's done more than heal me. In my helplessness, he has made me whole.

Reaching for Wonder

I've imagined what it might have been like for the paralyzed man who was healed by Jesus. It's a reasonable imagining, but I don't know if it's true. The Bible only tells us:

> Some people arrived, and four of them were bringing to him a man who was paralyzed. They couldn't carry him through the crowd, so they tore off part of the roof above where Jesus was. When they had made an opening, they lowered the mat on which the paralyzed man was lying. When Jesus saw their faith, he said to the paralytic, "Child, your sins are forgiven!" . . . "But so you will know that the Human One has authority on the earth to forgive sins"—he said to the man who was paralyzed, "Get up, take your mat, and go home." Jesus raised him up, and right away he picked up his mat and walked out in front of everybody. (Mark 2:3-5, 10-12a)

Through the whole narrative, the paralyzed man never speaks, Jesus never comments on his faith, and the man doesn't do a single thing until Jesus tells him to "Get up, take your mat, and go home." The nameless man picks up his mat and walks out. No words, no response, no indication of his emotional state or reactions. That itself tells us more, perhaps, than words ever could.

In his silence we see that not only can he not act for himself, he does not speak for himself either. He is paralyzed within as well as without. His inability to act, to even speak, emphasizes his utter helplessness.

I've been there, at least emotionally if not physically, where I'm helpless to help myself and I can't even articulate my need. I've been there after a doctor's appointment. I've been there in my child's room when I knew there was nothing more I could do. I've been there across the table from a friend when all I could do was cry and there were no words. I've been there lying in my own bed, my husband beside me, and the silence so heavy that I didn't think I would ever breathe again.

Sometimes the only way we can be healed is through letting others carry our mat, dig a hole, and place us in the presence of Jesus.

Helplessness. A child . . . a spouse . . . a boss . . . an incurable disease . . . there are places in life where we are paralyzed. They make us doubt our worth, they make us doubt our friends, our future, our God. We want to either wallow in our pain or snap our fingers and make it better. But sometimes "you can do anything you set your mind to" isn't true. Sometimes we are helpless. And helplessness hurts.

Yet the man on the mat tells us that at times silence and stillness are just the conditions that Jesus needs to make us whole.

I am reminded of the day I found Smokey, my husband's horse, standing still and silent in his stall. Smokey is never still and silent.

My daughter Bethany came into the barn. "What's wrong with Smokey?"

Smokey stared at us from behind his feeding net. We stepped closer. He didn't wiggle. He didn't whinny.

Bethany moved toward him. "Oh no." She glanced at me. "His hoof is caught in the net. He can't get it out." She slipped slowly into his stall, hoping not to spook him. She took his hoof in her hand.

"The fabric is wedged between his hoof and his shoe. I can't pull it out. If he starts to panic, he'll break his leg."

"OK, you keep him calm. I'll find something to cut the net."

For the next twenty minutes, we sawed and soothed and cut and calmed until Smokey was finally free. He couldn't move, he didn't speak, and he couldn't help himself. He just stayed still and let us work. Sometimes, in our fear, in our helplessness, that's all we have to do too. Sometimes God is whispering into our silence: "Be still, and know that I am God" (Psalm 46:10 KJV).

That's all the man on the mat had to do. Trust the right people, stay still, wait for God to work. Part the crowd.

But the first thing he needed was to let others carry his mat.

Let Others Carry Your Mat

Often, acknowledging helplessness is the hardest step of all. We like to be self-sufficient. We like to have a plan. We like to be in control. "I do it myself" is one of the first sentences most of my children ever spoke. And age doesn't dull the desire for independence.

We want him to heal our circumstances, our marriages, relationships, children, bodies, but often he needs to correct what's wrong inside us first.

But in the most difficult times of life, we, like the man on the mat, are often beyond self-reliance. We cannot do it ourselves. The paralyzed man couldn't even take himself out of bed, let alone take himself to Jesus. He couldn't carry his own mat, he couldn't walk to the house where Jesus was, and he couldn't move the crowd. There were barriers in his life that he couldn't overcome alone.

There are barriers in our lives also. And sometimes the only way around the barriers is a rooftop excursion and a hole big enough to lower us down. Sometimes the only way we can be healed is through letting others carry our mat, dig a hole, and place us in the presence of Jesus.

When Paul says, "Carry each other's burdens and so you will fulfill the law of Christ" (Galatians 6:2), he means that sometimes others must carry us to where we need to be and make a way when we are helpless to do so ourselves. Sometimes we are paralyzed on a mat and the crowd won't part and only strong friends can find another way. Friends can't heal us, but they can get us in front of Jesus. And when our faith fails, theirs can stand in the gap. Because all they need to do is have enough faith to get us to our Savior . . . especially when we are paralyzed, inside and out.

Paralyzed, Inside and Out

So what does it mean to be paralyzed inside and out? Outer paralysis is more obvious. We know we often do not have the power to fix our bodies, our circumstances, even our position in life through a simple 1-2-3 to-do list. We do not have the power to make the situation, or ourselves, whole in a physical sense. But internal paralysis is harder to see. It can fool us. It occurs when we can't speak truth to ourselves, and we can't articulate our hurt to God or others. We are caught in destructive patterns of thinking, and we can't move to where we need to be mentally, emotionally, or spiritually. We're stuck.

The paralyzed man was too. Writer and songwriter Michael Card says, "This story alludes to a complicated truth that is often oversimplified. Yes, there is a connection between sickness and sin. But no, not all sin leads to physical sickness. Not all sickness is a direct result of sin. Yet it is safe to say that all sin paralyzes."[1]

And that's the power of helplessness. It sets the stage for whole-person healing, based not on ourselves but on the wonder of God and how he reaches out to us when we cannot reach at all.

I think this is why Jesus forgives sin first. He heals the inner paralysis before he heals the outer. Although Psalm 103:3 says, "God forgives all your sins, heals all your sickness," this story in Mark 2 is the only recorded instance in which Jesus both forgives sin and heals a physical ailment in the same person.

Cyril of Alexandria, a church patriarch from the fifth century, wrote in his Commentary on Luke, Homily 12, "For those who believe in him, being healed of the diseases of the soul, will receive forgiveness of the sins which they formerly committed. He may also mean this: 'I must heal your soul before I heal your body. . . . Even though you have not asked for this, I as God see the maladies of the soul which brought on you this disease.'"[2]

Often, in our helplessness, God sees that he must heal the hurts of our souls before he can heal our external troubles. We want him to heal our circumstances, our marriages, relationships, children, bodies, but often he needs to correct what's wrong inside us first. The patterns that make us feel worthless, helpless, voiceless, hopeless need to be cleansed before outer healing can take hold. In Matthew 23:26, Jesus exhorts the Pharisees, "First clean the inside of the cup so that the outside of the cup will be clean too." In this story of a paralyzed man being lowered through a roof, Jesus shows us what that looks like. Through forgiveness he heals the inner paralysis first.

And then, only then, can he do the other impossible thing. He empowers the man to part the crowd.

Parting the Crowd

When the men first brought the paralyzed man to Jesus, they couldn't part the crowd. Not only could the friends not heal the man, they couldn't get the barriers to move out of their way. Instead, they had to climb to the roof, make a hole, and get their friend in front of Jesus. The man's need, his condition, his desperation couldn't get the attention of the people in their way.

The God who didn't heal a paralyzed man until a roof was torn open is not the God of the easy way. He never has been.

But once the man is in front of Jesus, Jesus not only heals him on the inside, then on the outside, but he also gives him the strength to part the crowd. It is the only thing the man does in this story. With Jesus's help, he gets up. He picks up his mat. And he walks through the formerly impenetrable crowd.

So it is with us. What was impossible becomes possible. In

our helplessness, God not only heals, he gives us ability to use the strength with which he gifts us to make a way where none was previously available.

And better yet, barriers turn into spokesmen for his glory. The crowd that had been an impermeable wall becomes a chorus for Jesus's praise as they murmur, "We've never seen anything like this."

The crowd barred the way. Now, they proclaim Christ's wonder.

And that's the power of helplessness. It sets the stage for whole-person healing, based not on ourselves but on the wonder of God and how he reaches out to us when we cannot reach at all. He pulls us to our feet, and only then can we part the crowd and hear the whispers of wonder.

Through the story of the paralyzed man on his mat, we encounter this God who turns helplessness into wonder. But he does it the hard way.

Who Is This God?

I tremble as I write that. I don't like the hard way. I like the easy, simple, or straightforward ways. But the God who didn't heal a paralyzed man until a roof was torn open is not the God of the easy way. He never has been.

This is a God who started the whole human race with a single couple and then allowed them the choice to eat from a tree that would ruin them. That's not the easy way.

This is a God who freed his people from four hundred years of slavery and led them, in their unfaithfulness, for forty years on a desert trek that could have taken less than two weeks.

This is the God who said to Gideon, "With the three hundred

men who lapped I will rescue you and hand over the Midianites to you. Let everyone else go home" (Judges 7:7) when Gideon started with thirty-two thousand. A fighting force of thirty-two thousand when going into battle is the easy way. Three hundred is not.

This is the God of David, who had to run and hide from a murderous King Saul after David was anointed by Samuel as king of Israel. God gave David victories in battle, but he did not give him the throne without years of running, hiding, separation from his best friend, and fear of the man he once served faithfully and loved like a father.

Even after the death, resurrection, and ascension of Jesus, God did not take the easy way. The early Christians were persecuted, stoned, imprisoned, and killed in gruesome ways. And in their suffering, the good news and hope of Christ spread throughout the Roman Empire.

It would have been easier for Jesus to fill his ranks with powerful political leaders. Instead, he called fishermen and tax collectors, prostitutes, and men lowered through rooftops. He called us. A few of us have power. A few wealth. But all of us, in so many ways, are helpless.

God takes us on the difficult path, the narrow way, the long, uphill road. But we don't travel alone. When we don't have faith enough for another step, God provides.

And God takes us the hard way.

But the hard way is not the impossible way. And in our

helplessness, God sends who we need. God created Eve when Adam needed a helpmate. God sent Moses and Joshua when the Israelites needed leaders to not only free them but lead them to God's Promised Land. Gideon had three hundred men. David had his warriors and the love of Saul's son, Jonathan.

Just as the paralyzed man had friends of faith who would not only carry his mat but also rip a hole in a roof for their helpless friend who could not even get up from his mat on his own.

God takes us on the difficult path, the narrow way, the long, uphill road. But we don't travel alone. When we don't have faith enough for another step, God provides. When we don't have hope enough to get ourselves where we need to be, God provides. When we're alone on our bed in the darkness before dawn and we can't move our arms, our legs, or our hearts, God is working to provide a way in our helplessness.

But that way may not look quite like we expect. Because sometimes God doesn't part the crowd. Sometimes he provides a thatched roof and unexpected hands to dig through it. Sometimes we have to be hauled to places we don't want to go and are afraid we may fall from. And sometimes, often, we have to take a rickety ride down a hole we can't see, held by the hands of others, in order to encounter the living God.

So trust the people who feed your hope and not your despair. Rely on those who are faithful when you cannot be. Let them tear a hole in the roof to bring you to Jesus. And then let Jesus see into your soul and do what must be done. Submit to the hard way. It is God's way.

Then the crowd will part, and in the encounter, you will hear the whispers, "We've never seen anything like this . . ."

*Lord, there are places in my life where I am helpless and hopeless.
There are crowds I cannot part, needs I cannot articulate, hopes I cannot even hope for. Help me, Lord, to trust, to be still, and to submit to your whole-person healing.
Help me to rest in you and whoever you send me in this "hard way" so I may walk again and hear the whispers of wonder.
"We've never seen anything like this . . ."*

When he saw her, the Lord had compassion for her and said, "Don't cry." He stepped forward and touched the stretcher on which the dead man was being carried. Those carrying him stood still. Jesus said, "Young man, I say to you, get up." The dead man sat up and began to speak, and Jesus gave him to his mother.

Luke 7:13-15

SEE ALSO LUKE 7:11-17.

4

Reaching Through Loss

A Widow's Dead Son

I used to skip this story. It seemed so small, so sparse. If I wanted to read about Jesus raising a man from the dead, the story of Lazarus was much more appealing.

I was wrong.

Here, tucked inconspicuously in the middle of the book of Luke, is a story of amazing hope for the "pile-on" phenomenon, for those times when losses rain down one after another like punches from a professional boxer until we're down for the count. When one staggering loss is too much, but more just keep coming.

What does it mean for us when we face loss after loss after loss and all we have left in our hearts, our souls, are the multi-toned cries of hurt and grief calling out within and behind us?

I wish I could say the pile-on phenomenon was rare. But it's not. I wish I could say that once you belong to God you'll only get as much as you can handle. But that's a lie. The Bible only says we won't be tempted more than we can bear. But loss? Suffering? Pain? There are no such guarantees for those.

The pile-on effect is real. And it's nothing new. We suffer from it now. And when Jesus walked the earth with his disciples, a widow from Nain suffered from it too.

It might have happened something like this:

~ A Widow Tells Her Story ~

I have lost everything. I lost my husband. I lost my only son. I lost my support, my security, my standing. I lost everyone I love. Now I lead this funeral procession of mourners. Of wailing and weeping. Of friends who care but will not be there when I am destitute. It is custom for me to lead this procession. It is custom for the crowd to follow. It is custom for the bier to be carried and the coffin open. It is custom for the crowd to cry. Today. Only today.

Rabbis have said, "Woman, who brought death into the world, ought to lead the way in the funeral procession."[1] So I lead it. And drown in the sound of sorrow. Each step echoes with finality, each tear uncounted, unseen by those behind me.

I lead a large crowd. And yet I am alone. I will always be alone.

There is nothing, no one, left for me now.

I shuffle toward Nain's main gate. Another crowd approaches it, opposite of mine. Opposite in so many ways. My crowd weeps. The other talks and laughs, their heads held high. There is an easiness, a swing in their steps. And the one who leads could not be more different from me. He doesn't weep and mourn. Tears don't wet his cheeks. His shoulders are not bent with the enormity of his pain.

Then, he sees me.

My footsteps slow. His countenance changes. Softens. Does he know I take my only son to the grave?

The two crowds meet at the gate and pause. Only he approaches. Only the one who sees me. And silence falls, as if the whole world is holding its breath.

Then comes his voice, gentle, strong. "Don't cry."

Don't cry? A strange command, an impossible one, to a woman who has lost everything. And yet . . . yet . . . in it I almost hear a glimmer of promise. How could it be?

He moves toward the dead body of my son. He looks like a rabbi, but like none I have ever known. I should call out, warn him not to touch what is dead. But words stick in my throat like dough taken too soon from the oven. He touches the bier that carries the body of my son. But no one calls out "unclean."

The pallbearers are still. We are all still. Two crowds, and no one says a single word. Except for him. And again he gives an impossible command.

"Young man," he says, "I say to you, get up!"

And there, in the coffin, my son rises. Murmurs ripple through the crowds.

I cannot speak. But my son does. He speaks to the man of God. I cannot hear his words. But I know one thing: he is alive. I don't know how. But he is alive!

Voices surge around me. Two crowds that have become one as they circle us.

"A great prophet has appeared among us!"

"God has come to help his people!"

This more-than-a-rabbi reaches for my son, helps him from the casket, brings him to me.

I wrap my arms around my living boy, and I weep with a different kind of weeping. He has given me back my son's life, but he has really given me back my own.

I had lost everything, but not everything is now lost.

I have my son. And I have more.

I have learned that even in the deepest loss, God has come to help his people. He came to help me.

And my crowd of mourners has merged with his to become a crowd of praise, of wonder.

Reaching for Wonder

Dead bodies and biers, clashing crowds and crying mothers. It seems to be a scene painted with only dark colors and pain. Until there is an encounter with Jesus. Until the crowd of those who represent the pile-on losses of a widow with a dead only-son meets the crowd led by Jesus. Then, the mourners are swallowed up and the power of loss broken.

How does this happen? What does it mean for us when we face loss after loss after loss and all we have left in our hearts, our souls, are the multi-toned cries of hurt and grief calling out within and behind us?

The widow's crowd of mourners was not an indication of support for her in her loss. Rather, as scholar David Garland says, "Accompanying a funeral procession was considered to be virtuous. . . . [The size of the crowd] should not be taken to imply, however, that the widow had a huge support network to help her survive in the days to come."[2] Despite the large crowd, the widow was a woman who had nothing left. Her life had become a series of losses until this point when there was nothing more left to lose. She was bereft.

All Is Lost

When I approach this funeral procession for the only son of a widow, I am struck by how much she had suffered to this point. She was a widow, so she had lost her husband, which means she had lost her fertility, the ability to have more children. Then, she lost her only son, her child. Isn't that more than enough? But she also lost her care, her societal position, her security, her place in the community, and her source of living. Childless widows were the most desperate people in her society.

God didn't keep her husband from dying. He didn't give her more sons. And, finally, her only son died as well.

What does an encounter with the living God look like, what difference does it make, when the losses have piled up so high that you cannot see over them? Or when it seems that God has arrived too late, far too late?

I remember struggling with these questions not for myself, but for my daughter, a few years ago.

When Joelle was eight she fell in love with a young rescue pony at an adoption event. His name was Squishy and he was small and gangly. He looked like a bunch of body parts tossed together by a blindfolded monkey.

What does an encounter with the living God look like, what difference does it make, when the losses have piled up so high that you cannot see over them?

He was too young to be trained and we had no place to put him. So we walked away. But Joelle never forgot Squishy. She drew pictures of him to cover the walls of her room. She talked about him. She dreamt about him.

Two years later, Squishy was still small and gangly. But now, he was old enough to be trained. So we made a place for him at our ranch.

Joelle was so excited. She wrote books and illustrated them to sell to her grandma's friends. She did chores for others, jobs for her dad, anything to earn the three-hundred-dollar adoption fee for Squishy. So, in time, we brought him home.

And Joelle trained him, loved him, cared for him.

Until the morning when we went out to the barn to find him upside down, his leg broken, his hoof caught in the top of the fence in a freak accident. Joelle lost her pony that morning.

That evening she lost her pet rat.

The next morning, she went to school for the first time without her best friend, who had moved to the other side of the country during their break.

Loss upon loss upon loss, for a little girl whose heart had been tender and now was broken over, and over, and over.

I had no words of comfort. I had no pat answers. I couldn't make it better. All I could do was mourn, like the crowd who followed the widow as she took her dead son to the grave. All I could do was trust that somehow, Christ would meet us at the gate and that would make a difference.

Confrontation of Crowds

When we suffer multiple losses, multiple blows in our lives, we cannot expect a simple recovery. We carry with us not just a single sorrow, a simple hurt. Rather, we have a crowd of mourners, as we should. Our mourners may not all be physical, but could be emotional and mental, such as thoughts that plague us or emotions that dog our steps even when we want to just bury our dead and move on. What do we do with this crowd of sorrows, doubts, and disappointments that are mixed with anger, hopelessness, hurt, and despair?

The cries of these members of the crowd are to be expected as much as mourners at the funeral of a widow's dead son. It is custom for all these emotions and struggles to trail us, wailing, as we walk to the grave.

But ours is not the only crowd at the scene. Jesus brings his own crowd to meet us, a crowd very different from the one that follows us when we're experiencing a pile-on.

His crowd meets ours at the gate of the city. In the confrontation, the meeting of these two crowds, Jesus brings to ours enough power, intention, and compassion to not just silence it but to transform it.

In the Middle East of Jesus's day, the gate was a crossroads of sorts. Inside was safe, familiar, protected from marauders and attackers. Outside you could meet anybody. Outside the world wasn't safe, wasn't predictable. Jesus often meets us precisely at the gate, where life has been shaken up and it isn't safe anymore. He meets us when we don't know what will happen to us, what we'll meet "out there," and yet we have no choice but to leave the safety of our city and take our dead hopes and dreams to the graveyard outside the walls.

It's there, at the uncomfortable place between safety and uncertainty, that Jesus encounters us and our crowd. And as with the widow, there is this moment when Jesus looks at us with compassion. He sees us, not just in a glance but in looks that expose our souls. He sees our sorrow, doubts, and despair. And he doesn't judge. He doesn't condemn or sneer. Rather, he is filled with compassion and he moves toward us.

At that point, the choice is ours. We are faced with the question of whether we will allow the pallbearers to stop. Will we allow Jesus to approach the worst of our pain? Will we allow him to touch the dead parts of our life, our hope, our soul?

Our doubts, our disappointments, our anger, our despair—they aren't too much for Jesus to handle. We must bring them all to the gate. We must allow his crowd and ours to come face-to-face with each other. We cannot hide our crowd, we cannot pretend the two crowds are the same.

In the face of the pile-on, the question is whether we will stop and allow Jesus to encounter us at the gate.

All Is Not Lost

The widow chooses to stop. And wait. That's all she must do. She doesn't have to muster enough faith. She doesn't have to disband her crowd or get them all lined up in a row, looking good. She doesn't have to pretend they don't exist or that she's going to be OK. She just needs to stop and wait for what Jesus will do.

Will we allow Jesus to approach the worst of our pain? Will we allow him to touch the dead parts of our life, our hope, our soul?

And what he does first seems rather odd. He issues an impossible invitation. He says to her, "Don't cry." At first, this may seem like an insensitive comment, but given that the text directly precedes his command with "the Lord had compassion for her" (v. 13), we know these words are not a rebuke but an invitation to hope again, to hope against all hope, to let Jesus come near. And to let him touch the bier of death.

Sometimes, that's what Jesus is saying to us too. He's not bidding us to get up enough faith to drown our own fears and sorrows, he is only inviting us to dare to hope, just enough to allow him to draw near and touch the places of death in our lives.

Something amazing happens when we do. Something filled with a new kind of wonder. For the widow, her son was raised from the dead. But something else happened too. Something also unexpected, something also filled with wonder.

Her crowd of mourners mixed with the crowd following Jesus and became one with them. Verse 16 tells us, "Awestruck, *everyone* praised God" (emphasis mine). Everyone. There was no longer a distinction between the two crowds. Now, it was one crowd, all praising Jesus. "A great prophet has appeared among us," they said. "God has come to help his people." God has come!

At the gates in our lives, Jesus does not promise to fix all our problems. But he does promise his presence, and he promises this miracle of our crowd of mourners transforming into a crowd of praise and wonder. It may not happen through a physical raising of the dead, of restoring our lives to just what they were before, but through his own death and resurrection we can be assured that Jesus can redeem the dead parts of our lives and bring amazing new life where we've only experienced death.

When we lost Squishy and Paris, the rat, and Joelle's best friend moved away, God didn't raise either the horse or the rat from the dead. Joelle's friend, Laura, didn't move back to town.

But other things happened that let us know that God saw, had compassion, and was moving to help and heal. When Marlene, the director of the horse rescue from whom we'd adopted Squishy, found out about his death, she called me. She told me she had a beautiful young mare that they'd rescued five months ago. And for five months, every time she looked at that horse, she thought of us and something in her heart stirred to tell her that horse should be ours. She never mentioned it because she knew we had enough horses. We didn't need another. But now, if Joelle wanted her, Marlene would give my daughter this beautiful mare with no adoption fee, no costs at all. Just a gift for a grieving girl who had experienced a pile-on.

And while Blizzard couldn't replace Squishy, she did touch that dead and hurting place in my daughter's heart, in all of our hearts, and bring life and healing and hope. And God put this gift into motion five months before Squishy died. God didn't prevent Squishy's death, but he did plan to meet us at the gate with compassion and a touch that would help heal.

Jesus planned to meet the widow too. Verse 11 says, "Jesus went to a city called Nain." Jesus didn't just happen to meet this woman and her mourners. He chose to go to Nain. He chooses to come to us too. He plans to arrive at just the right moment, just as we reach the gate.

Sometimes, we just haven't reached that gate yet. Sometimes we're still staggering in front of the crowd. Keep moving, step by step, stumble by stumble. He is coming to the gate, and he holds in his hands the hope to transform our crowd of mourners into a crowd which proclaims, "God has come to help his people."

Death and loss do not have the final say, even in the pile-on.

Who Is This God?

Our God is the God of the Pile-On. It doesn't surprise him, it doesn't shake him. Nor is it his method of punishment or proof that he doesn't care. We know that not only from the raising of the widow's son, but also from the book of Job.

For if God is the God of the Pile-On, then Job is its patron saint.

The opening of the book of Job tells us that Job was a righteous man with whom God was pleased. But God also allowed the Adversary to afflict pile-on pain on Job. Job lost his oxen, his donkeys, and his servants who cared for them. He also lost his sheep and his shepherds. He lost his camels and their caretakers. And then he lost all of his ten children. That was a pile-on. But it wasn't finished.

Job then lost his health. Job 2:7 says, "The Adversary . . . struck Job with severe sores from the sole of his foot to the top of his head." Then, "Job took a piece of broken pottery to scratch himself and sat down on a mound of ashes" (Job 2:8).

Through his own death and resurrection we can be assured that Jesus can redeem the dead parts of our lives and bring amazing new life where we've only experienced death.

Next, the crowd of mourners came. His wife urged him to "curse God and die." His friends sat with him and then began to insist that the pile-on was his punishment for his sin. Job insisted it was not. But he brought his own crowd of doubts and despair, of cursing the day of his birth and calling out to God to explain this pain, to justify it.

But God did not meet Job's crowd with explanations. He met it with his presence. God appeared to Job in a whirlwind. The whirlwind was the gate in which Job could encounter God. And in the whirlwind, God brought a crowd of images of his glory. Great images of morning stars that sing, a sea bursting forth, the expanses of earth and the storehouses of hail. Intimate images of feeding lion cubs and hungry raven chicks, mountain goats giving birth, and wild donkeys set free.

And in the whirlwind, where the crowds met, somehow Job's crowd was transformed into a mouth-covering wonder. "My ears had heard about you," Job says in 42:5-6, "but now my eyes have seen you. Therefore, I relent and find comfort."

Later we find that Job lived many more years and was "old and satisfied" (Job 42:17). He was satisfied not, as some argue, because God restored his fortunes and allowed him to have more children (anyone who has lost a child knows that new children cannot erase the pain of losing a child), but because Job encountered God in the whirlwind and somehow God was able to touch those dead places in him so that his crowd could proclaim, "God has come to help his people."

God came. God healed. Even in the pile-on.

God wants to touch the deep things in us as well and bring them back to life. He wants to heal those places in our souls that we are sure are dead because of our piled-on pain. When we're down for the count, when there's so much loss that we can't breathe beneath it all, Jesus comes to the place that is not familiar, that doesn't feel safe. He wants to encounter us there and bring our dead places to life again.

We will hope again and breathe again, our dead hopes and dreams can be resurrected by his hand, because he meets us at the city gate when we have a dead body on the bier. He looks with compassion. And he wants to touch the deep places of death within us.

Will we back away from the gate? Or will we meet him there?

Lord, in the pile-ons of life help me to trust
that you will meet me at the gate.
Help me to be still and allow you to touch the dead places within me.
I know that you have come to help your people, to help me.
May I be brave enough to keep going until I can encounter you at the
gate, in the whirlwind.

Jesus asked him, "What is your name?"
He responded, "Legion is my name, because we are many."

Mark 5:9

See also Mark 5:1-20; Matthew 8; Luke 8.

5

REACHING THROUGH THE VOICES WITHIN

We Are Legion

Few stories are more fascinating than the tale of a man who had a legion of demons. Sometimes when we speak of demons in the New Testament, people want to argue about whether demons are real or if they are but forms of mental illness. Some want to debate how many demons can fit on the head of pin, or in this case, in one poor man. Others want to focus on the question of whether Christians are immune to possession.

But no matter the debates, none of us are immune to the voices in our heads. We all know the whispers that arise in our minds when life turns to dark, painful places. All of us can relate to the pressures of insidious thoughts that are not from God and mean only to destroy us. Thoughts that tell us we're worthless, hated, unable, unfit, unwanted, abandoned, helpless, hopeless, and no one, even God, can redeem us. Thoughts that drive us to actions we despise and cause us to hurt those around us. Voices that build hate and fury, that break community, crush love, and leave us lonely.

*I wonder . . . what is it like to encounter
Christ when the voices are so loud you can
no longer hear yourself think or pray or
believe?*

You know those thoughts. You know the chaos they create within you. I do too.

They drive us from ourselves and from others. But they cannot drive us from Jesus. The story of the man with a legion of demons tells us that. So I look to this man with thousands of voices screaming for attention in his mind, and I wonder . . . what is it like to encounter Christ when the voices are so loud you can no longer hear yourself think or pray or believe? Can Jesus reach through the voices within? Can he silence them? And if he does, will we hear the very voice of God?

Let's travel with the demoniac to the edge of the Sea of Galilee. Let us bring our inner voices, the lies we believe and act on, the fears that eat our souls, and see what happens when those voices encounter the powerful presence of God.

It may have happened something like this:

~ A Demoniac Tells His Story ~

He comes. I see. I see him. Down the shore. Across the water. Water shimmers. He is on it. Calm. No storm. There was a storm. They sent it. The ones in me. The voices. The voices sent a storm. Didn't stop him. Didn't drown it. I wanted to drown him. No, not me. Them. They didn't. Couldn't. Fear. Anger. Screaming in my head. Water is too calm. Boat glides. Toward shore. Toward me. Us. He comes. Yes, he comes. To my shore. I pant. I tear my hair. There is no pain. Should be pain. They laugh. They shriek.

Hatred. Fury. The endless roiling of voices and thoughts and horror.

And the man on the shore. Won't come to tombs. No one comes to tombs. I see him from tombs. My tombs. They see him.

They see the man on the shore. Others too. So few.

I am many. No one can bind me. No one can subdue me, capture me, control me. No one but them. They cut me, strip me, until I howl to the hills in my anguish. I am many.

He is more.

They know. I don't know.

Run. I should run. Away.

I run. Closer. Not away. I run to the man. Man on the shore.

They drive me toward him. I stumble. I run. My feet pound the ground. I hear the voices. I hear the thudding of my feet. I hear the cries and shrieks and maddening terror. I would tear my clothes but I have none. I am an animal. I am a vessel. I hold the voices within.

They gnash and shout and scream.

Then I am falling. Not falling. I am on my knees.

Before him.

Him.

I cannot look at him. He looks at me.

I hate him. I hate him! I hear their hisses. I hear their shouts. "What have you to do with me, Jesus, Son of the Most High God? Swear to God that you won't torture me!" My mouth moves. I don't speak. They speak. They always speak. No one hears me. They don't hear me scream.

I hear me.

He hears me too?

"Unclean spirit, come out of the man!"

I writhe within. Hate. Fear. Voices. So many voices.

But I can still hear him. "What is your name?" he asks. He doesn't shout. He doesn't even raise his voice.

My mouth moves again, as if commanded by him. I must speak. They must speak. "Legion is my name," they whisper with a guttural sound, "because we are many."

Truth. They must speak the truth. I feel them quaking within me. Afraid. So very afraid. Powerless. Legion, they say. Many. They are many. So very, very many. They use a term of battle, of war. Why battle? They have already won. Unless . . .

"Send us into the pigs! Let us go into the pigs!" They all cry out with the same request. Slithering voices. So much fear.

I have a thought. A single, clear thought. My soul is weeping. I hear its cry. *Set me free, strange man on the shore. Free me from these voices in my head, my heart, my soul.*

"Go."

And then they are gone. There is silence within me. Blessed, beautiful silence. Outside, I hear the squeal of pigs, the splash and tumble of water, the gasp of the others who are with this man who freed me. I hear the wind and water and feet of the pig-herders who rush toward us. And I hear myself. My whole mind is clear. I can hear my own voice again.

Someone hands me a robe. He helps me to don it. I feel the soft fabric against my skin. I feel warmth and the gentle touch of the man who helps dress me. I run my hands through my hair and shift my legs until I am sitting at the feet of the One who freed me.

He leans down and speaks healing words meant only for my ears. I hear him so clearly. Not only in my ears, but in my very soul. His voice is like a song.

The pig herders rush away. I don't care. I just want to sit at his feet. I just want to listen to his voice. His singular voice that speaks to every part of me and makes me whole. So I sit, and listen, and rejoice in the quietness within and without.

Soon, villagers return with the pig herders. I recognize them. They are the ones who tried to bind me, control me, even help me. But they could not do what this man on the shore has done.

And they know it.

They come forward, trembling as they see me fully dressed and in my right mind. They are afraid. I will never be afraid again. Never. I hear the pig herders whisper about what happened to the pigs, pointing to the place where the swine tumbled into the sea.

The villagers whisper their awe, and their fear. And for a moment, I am reminded of other voices.

Then one steps forward, speaks to the man who freed me. "Please, leave our region," he pleads.

Why would he ask such a thing? Why are they so afraid? Almost as afraid as the voices that once drove me mad.

The man on the shore turns and motions his men to follow. They walk toward the water. They step into the boats.

I jump up and run toward them, toward him. "Please, I beg you, let me join you. Let me be one of your disciples, your followers."

He smiles at me with a kindness, a mercy, more than I have ever known. "No," he says. "Go home to your own people and tell them what the Lord has done for you and how he has shown you mercy."

I meet his eyes, and I nod. I will do whatever he tells me. He has restored me to myself. Now, he will restore me to those I once loved. He will restore me to my community.

I turn from him and walk away. The villagers have already started their journey back to town. I follow them, reveling in the quiet peace in my mind.

There are no more voices within, except for mine . . . and his.

Reaching for Wonder

What if the voices inside our heads were only our own and God's? What if the voices that accused, condemned, lied, and attacked were cast out and silenced? What if the things we told ourselves in secret were the very words of God? I want to live that way. I want to be freed.

But I know, like the demoniac knew, that life with the wrong voices in your head is no life at all. In three verses, Mark 5:3-5, we see how every part of the demoniac's life had been destroyed by the demons living within him. First, he lived among the tombs. He resided in the place of death, decay, horror, and those beyond hope or help. He was completely cut off from his community, from anyone who might show him kindness, gentleness, love. Only the dead and the demons were with him.

Only he can cast out the destructive voices within us.

They had broken his chances for any human help. No one was strong enough to restrain him. No one could hold him, so no one could help him. Neither chains nor leg irons, let alone ropes, could subdue him enough to remain around people.

He had no home but the tombs and the hills. He was naked, stripped of even the clothing that would identify him as a human. Scholar David Garland writes, "Jesus meets a demonized man who wears no clothes, a sign of his shame and loss of identity."[1]

He hurt others. He hurt himself. He cut himself with stones. The voices were so strong, so inescapable, that he was driven to self-harm, to the scream of pain . . . and even that did not silence the voices within.

So he became like an animal, howling night and day. Troubled, without rest, day after night after day after night with no bed, no clothes, no home, no friends, no family, no chance . . . except one.

Except this stranger on the shore.

The presence of Jesus brings evil to the light. And when it is revealed, Jesus calls it to come out, of the demoniac and out of us.

Only he could cast out the voices that drove the demoniac to destruction. Only he can cast out the destructive voices within us as well.

They Make Themselves Known

We know what the voices say. Perhaps his said, "You're worthless, you're an animal, you're bad, evil, irredeemable." So like the condemning voices in our heads. "You're not good enough. You're so stupid. You're fat, you're ugly. Those people hate you. . . . You're shamed and despised. You're less than. They're less than. You're different. You're wrong. They're wrong. You can never be free. You can never be who God created you to be."

Lies.

But they will not be silent on their own. And sometimes that's not a bad thing.

Because there's one thing about these voices in the demoniac's head, in our heads, that leads to their ruin: they make themselves known. They don't run and hide.

When Jesus arrived on the shore of the Sea of Galilee, the demoniac didn't hide in the tombs or in the hills. He didn't run in the other direction, even though Jesus had just defeated and calmed the storm on the sea. Instead, he, and all his inner voices, ran straight to Jesus. Mark 5:2 tells us, "And when Jesus had stepped out of the boat, immediately there met him out of the tombs a man with an unclean spirit" (ESV).

The presence of Jesus brings evil to the light. And when it is revealed, Jesus calls it to come out, of the demoniac and out of us.

Every ungodly thought, every whispered accusation that comes from the evil one, every voice that does not reflect the truth of God, all are exposed by Jesus. And when they are exposed, we can know them by name.

When Jesus asks, "What is your name?" the demons cannot help replying, "My name is Legion, for we are many" (v. 9 ESV). The name *Legion* is a military term. They have conquered this man. They believe they've defeated him.

When Jesus shines the light of truth on the voices within, they are revealed for what they really are. They come to him, like Legion, ready to fall into formation and fight. But with Jesus, they have no power. The voices only have power when they whisper within us. In an encounter with Jesus, they have no power over us at all. "Send us to the pigs; let us enter them," they plead (v. 12 ESV). When confronted by Jesus, they are already defeated. They are already at his mercy, to do with whatever he chooses.

He chooses to send them into the pigs.

Into the Pigs

Why pigs? In Jewish culture and law, pigs are unclean, unholy. Not only were Israelites commanded to not eat the pig, the whole culture demanded that pigs be avoided and disdained. By casting the demons into the pigs, Jesus very literally shows that these demons, and therefore the thoughts they whispered into the demoniac's mind, were unclean, unholy, and should have nothing to do with God's chosen people. They should have nothing to do with you and me. The voices that come not from God but from the evil one are unclean and unholy. They belong in pigs, not in us. And that's just where God intends them to be. We need not be subject to the unholy voices within us.

The pigs then rush down the cliff into the lake and drown. Pigs are not lemmings. This is not their normal behavior. They've wandered these same hills often before and never behaved this way. But when the demons enter them, they all run over the cliff and die. The unclean voices within us drive us to do things that are uncharacteristic and lead to our destruction. What the demons did to the pigs they intended to do to the man. Every whisper, every stealthy hiss, every sharp shout was intended to drive him to death and destruction. The dark forces that battle to control us, the voices that haunt us in our worst moments, the thoughts within that confuse and cause us to hurt others and ourselves—their goal is always the same: our death, to destroy us.

These unclean thoughts do not belong in a mind dedicated to Jesus. But we cannot cast them out ourselves. Others cannot bind them for us. Instead, we must encounter Christ and throw ourselves at his feet. Only he can free us from the lies the enemy tries to plant in our minds and hearts. Only he can send them into the pigs.

REACHING THROUGH THE VOICES WITHIN

So what more can we do? We can only follow Paul's example when he says in 2 Corinthians 10:5 (NIV), "We take captive every thought to make it obedient to Christ." Every thought brought to Christ. Submitted to him. That's all we can do.

But it is enough. Because he is enough.

In His Right Mind

The villagers come to the scene and find something that scares them more than a man with a legion of demons. They find that man completely cured, dressed, and in his right mind. They also find two thousand dead pigs floating in the Sea of Galilee.

And they are terrified.

The man, however, is not. Instead, he is sitting at Jesus's feet, right where he should be, and he is fully clothed, signifying that his humanity has been restored, he has again become the person he was created to be.

We can only be where we need to be and be who we need to be when the unholy voices in our minds are silenced and cast out.

We must encounter Christ and throw ourselves at his feet. Only he can free us from the lies the enemy tries to plant in our minds and hearts.

When we can hear Jesus's voice again and speak with our own, then we can become a liaison between Christ and our community. The villagers were so afraid of Jesus that they asked him to leave their country. So he did. The man asked to go with Jesus, but instead Jesus told him to "Go home to your own people, . . . and tell them what the Lord has done for you and how he has shown you mercy" (v. 19).

To your own people. He who had no people now has a community. Jesus re-establishes him in his community and sends him with a message of hope that they could not hear from Jesus. They could only hear from this man.

Tell them. He who had no voice but that of demons, no words but only howls, now carries the very message of God to ten cities. And when Jesus returns to those cities again in Mark 7:31-37 he will encounter faith where there was once only fear.

What the Lord has done for you. As David Garland says, "Jesus did what this man or his community could not do by their own power. He broke the bonds of demons that held him fast."[2]

How he has shown you mercy. Jesus did more than cast out a legion of demons. He restored to this man more than he'd ever had before, and "everyone was amazed" (5:20). Wonder was born because, in a single encounter with the living God, Jesus replaced a legion of voices with his own.

And so it is with us. All the voices of fear, hate, despair, and desperation must be driven out. And in the silence, we hear his "still, small voice" (1 Kings 19:12 KJV). We hear the voice of God conversing with our own. And we are restored.

I know because I've seen it happen before my very eyes. A close friend began to believe the lies and fears whispered in her mind. She believed she was less than, not good enough, unloved. Then a man came into her life who enticed and tempted and lured her toward destructive behavior and isolation from everyone who loved her.

Her friends tried to help, but just like the demoniac, she broke the bonds that would have held her away from him. We were powerless to save her.

So we prayed. All we could do was pray.

And one night Jesus showed up on the shore. In a scene reminiscent of Mark 5, the man blurted out his malicious intentions to isolate her and have her for himself. He spoke of his plans, his needs, his desires. And through this, Jesus revealed to her that all those things that had been whispered in the dark were not words of love, instead they were fit only for pigs. They were meant for her death and destruction. Their purpose was to take everything away that made her beautiful and unique, human, to separate her from her community, devour her and her future.

But in a moment, God changed all that. The veil was removed from her eyes and she could see the lies for what they were. She could see the man for what he was. She was in her right mind again. That night, Jesus cast out not only the unhealthy voices within her but also the man who had tried to enslave her. He tried to come back, tried to lure her again, but he had no power. The pigs were dead.

When she was freed and restored, she became again the woman we all knew and loved. The unique personality traits that God had created in her bloomed and came to life again, stronger and more beautiful than before. She became a witness to God's mercy, and because of her, today my faith is stronger, my hope more resilient, my heart, like the hearts of those in the Ten Cities, more ready to receive God's truth when he visits again.

The voices have no power when you kneel before Jesus. Our God is the God of the voices within.

Who Is This God?

He is also the God of the Voice within. The one voice, the singular clear voice who created us each uniquely and speaks to us words of love, power, and self-control. Second Timothy 1:7 says, "God didn't give us a spirit that is timid but one that is powerful, loving, and self-controlled." That is who we are, who we are meant to be, who we become when we listen to the one voice instead of the many.

It has always been so.

Abraham heard the one voice in Ur, and had the faith to travel to the Promised Land and become the father of the nation of God, against all odds. He listened to God's voice, God's promises, and knew who he was. And became who he was meant to be.

In our worst moments, in our darkest times, in our helplessness and our hopelessness, isn't it time to meet Jesus on the shore after the storm? Isn't it time to be free?

Moses took off his shoes and listened to the voice in the burning bush. God's voice drove out his timidity, and Moses led the people of Israel out of slavery. God called Moses to be the leader of his people. Moses listened and became who he was meant to be.

David was chosen by God to be king of Israel. He persevered through death threats and being driven from his home because he listened to the voice of God and he knew who God called him to be. David became who he was meant to be, not only king but ancestor of the Messiah.

Peter, John, Andrew, James, they all listened to the one voice that called them to leave their nets and follow him. They became the disciples, the apostles, they were meant to be. They became fishers of men.

Paul heard the one voice on the road to Damascus. There, Jesus cast out the voices of hate and Paul listened to the clear call of his Savior. He became the missionary and epistle-writer he was meant to be.

Isn't it time we, too, brought the voices of doubt, fear, self-incrimination, others-incrimination, blame, hate, and every thought that is not of God, to Christ and allowed him to throw them out into the pigs until we can, finally, hear him, and him only, in our hearts, in our souls? Isn't it time to become who we were created to be?

In our worst moments, in our darkest times, in our helplessness and our hopelessness, isn't it time to meet Jesus on the shore after the storm? Isn't it time to be free?

Lord, help me to leave my tombs and run to you at the edge of the sea.
I kneel before you, powerless to silence these voices
that condemn and torment me.
Free me, Lord, cast out the thoughts that are not from you.
I bring them to you and hold them before you.
Fill me with your voice instead of theirs.
Make me be in my right mind again.

If I can just touch his clothes, I'll be healed.

Mark 5:28

SEE ALSO MARK 5:25-34; MATTHEW 9; LUKE 8.

6

REACHING THROUGH DESPERATION

The End of His Cloak

Just a little bit. That's all we ask for. Just a touch at the edge of his cloak. Just to stop the bleeding. Just to sneak through the crowd and make the pain cease. Just the minimum.

That would be enough for us. *Please, God, make it stop, make it go away, make it hurt a little less.* How many times have I prayed that prayer? About infertility, about kidney stones, about relational pain, about all the things that make me weary and hopeless and afraid. Just make it stop.

Christ's encounter with a woman who had been bleeding for twelve years makes me wonder if my prayers are simply too small.

The prayer makes sense. It's what I need. It's what my heart cries out for. And yet, while it may be enough for me, is it enough for

Jesus? Is he looking to give me, to give us, just a touch of his cloak, the very tiniest brush of our fingers against a tassel?

Or is there more? Should there be more? Christ's encounter with a woman who had been bleeding for twelve years makes me wonder if my prayers are simply too small.

Perhaps it happened like this:

A Bleeding Woman Tells Her Story

I've tried everything. Every physician, every treatment, every process of thought and prayer. And still I bleed. Twelve years. Twelve long years I've bled until I have no friends, no family, no more money left after paying doctors for treatments that only made the suffering worse. I am pale now, weak. I force myself out of bed every morning. Every day I fight a battle to live one more day. I fight alone.

Today is no different. Earlier, I rose, reluctantly, from my tattered bed. My legs shook in their weakness. I stumbled to the pile of clean rags and replaced the dirty ones from the night. I gathered the filthy strips of cloth, tucked them in the washing bowl, and ate my stale bread, a few lentils, and one dried fig. They tasted like dirt. Everything tastes like dirt. I ate anyway, slowly, chewing each bite and wishing that I could have one day, just one day, without the bleeding, without the pain, without the weariness.

But today began just like any other. I tidied my room, took my bowl, and dragged myself into the street. I slipped behind the houses, avoided the merchants, quietly made my way to the edge of the Sea of Galilee. Just like every day. And just like every day I now crouch at the edge of the water and clean the rags of my desperation. I scrub and rise, scrub and rest, scrub and dirty a whole new set as I clean the old. Others are at the sea, further down from me. No one looks at me. No one touches me. No one notices me anymore.

Sometimes that's a blessing.

Sometimes it's a curse.

If it would just stop. If I could just not bleed Every. Single. Day. If only the pain would lessen and I could return to my normal life. Everything wasn't perfect then, but it was enough. It was enough for me.

I straighten, stretch my back, and feel another gush of blood.

I close my eyes. Pull in a shuddering breath. If there were another treatment, I'd try it. If there were another doctor, I'd beg for his help. If there were anything I could do to make it stop, I would do it.

I am desperate, but I have run out of options.

Voices call out in the distance. The rumble of their words jumbles across the water. I open my eyes. A boat drifts closer. A crowd of townspeople hurry to meet it, to pull it all the way onto the shore. The men in the boat stand. One steps out. I recognize him. He is that Jesus. I heard him teach in parables. Soils and seeds, lamps and measures. I have no lamp anymore. And I am too weary to know anything about dirt, stones, and weeds.

We didn't understand his teachings. We still don't. And yet so many crowd around him now. I see the synagogue leader approach him and fall at his feet. Jesus touches the man's shoulder, bends to look in his face. I cannot hear what Jairus is saying. But I know his daughter is deathly ill. Is he asking the rabbi to heal her? The child was born the same month I started to bleed. She was a beautiful baby. I saw her once before I became unclean.

Jesus lifts his arm toward town, as if asking Jairus to lead the way. Jairus rises, and I see his face. I see the desperation. I see the hope.

And suddenly, I hope too. I know that desperation. I want to know that hope.

The crowd moves toward town. They walk quickly.

Do I dare? Do I dare try to follow? Someone may touch me in my uncleanness. But what *if* . . . what *if* I could just brush my fingers against his cloak and be healed? What *if*, when I touched him, he did not become unclean but instead I became clean? It's a wild thought, an audacious one. But somehow I cannot imagine he will be tainted by the slightest touch of my fingers on his hem.

I drop my bowl, my rags, and follow them.

My head is covered. I sneak closer. I am at the edge of the crowd. I am within it. I am closer, closer. So many people, so much jostling. Conversations and murmurings, footsteps and dust. The smell of bodies and the sea. He will never know if I just bend down and let my fingers graze the tassel of his prayer shawl. If I just touch his clothes I will be healed. I will be. It's all I've wanted for twelve long years.

I hold my hope like a precious jewel in trembling fingers. I hold my faith and I dare.

I dare to touch him.

My hand reaches out. The cloth tickles my skin. Just the slightest brush of my fingertips.

And strength flows through me.

I feel the healing in every part of me. The bleeding has stopped. I know it without needing to check. Power flows through my body, it pumps with the blood that no longer escapes.

I have everything I came for. Everything I wanted. My uncleanness is gone, washed away by his power. He is left untainted. I am left healed and clean.

I slip back into the crowd.

And he stops.

He turns.

The whole crowd stops with him.

And I am afraid.

His gaze sweeps the faces around him. "Who touched my clothes?"

I crouch down, and look away.

Jesus keeps looking. Looking for me.

I am shaking again, but not from weakness. I shake with fear, and with glory. I tremble because I know I am healed and I cannot just disappear. Healing was enough for me.

I see now that it is not enough for him.

I come forward, and like Jairus at the edge of the sea, I too fall at his feet. And I tell him what has happened to me. I tell him of my misery and of my hope. I tell him of weakness and my desperation. I tell him of my healing. I speak of the wonder he has given me.

But he has not given me all he wants to give.

He leans over, lifts my chin with two fingers, looks into my eyes. "Daughter," he says. He said it so gently. He called me daughter. And I am restored into a family again. His family. The family of his God, and mine.

"Your faith has healed you." And with those words, I am restored into the community of faith. I was invisible. I wove through a crowd that never saw me. They see me now. And through me, they see him; more than a rabbi, more than a healer who cannot be unclean, more than any of us ever dared to dream.

"Go in peace and be freed from your suffering" (Mark 5:34 NIV). Peace and freedom. All I wanted was healing. But he has given me more. He has healed more than the bleeding; he has healed my very soul.

I rise with tears pooling, slipping down my cheeks.

And now I see, now I know, healing is never enough. For me to be free, he had to call me daughter. He had to give me himself.

He stopped the crowd so that I could be more than healed, so I could be free.

Reaching for Wonder

As I write this, I am tired. I am weary. I am desperate for relief. Dear friends are planning to divorce, a family member just stormed off after a heated argument, my son's blood sugar is out of range, my daughter's beloved bunny is desperately sick, and my horse was just diagnosed with pigeon fever. And I find myself praying, "Just make it stop, Lord. Fix it! Just a moment of relief." In my exhaustion, in my desperation, all I can reach for is the smaller request.

Like the bleeding woman, I have exhausted all avenues, spent myself dry, tried everything, and right now, it only seems to have gotten worse. All I want is healing, a quick and final fix. But I need more than "make it better." I need Jesus. I need him to look me in the eye and say, as he did in Matthew's telling of this story (Matthew 9:20-22), "Take heart, daughter . . ." (NIV).

But that seems like too much to ask. I want just enough. I only want the edge of his cloak. Just the smallest touch to make me OK again. In my desperation, in my overwhelmed weariness, "OK" is good enough.

OK Is Not OK

What do we do when all we want is healing, but the more we pray the worse things seem to become? Usually we convince ourselves to settle for less.

It was good enough for the woman who bled for twelve years, too. She had spent everything and had only gotten worse. Her condition most likely caused severe anemia, so she must have been constantly exhausted. And her bleeding made her unclean, so no one would be able to touch her without becoming unclean themselves. No money, no energy, no human touch.

And then she sees a chance. She sees Jesus, the healer. But approaching him is a risk. She will have to risk being touched in the jostling crowd. She will have to risk being recognized. She will have to risk the wrath of making a rabbi unclean. But she believes that just the slightest brush of her fingers against his clothes will heal her.

I have exhausted all avenues, spent myself dry, tried everything, and right now, it only seems to have gotten worse. All I want is healing, a quick and final fix. But I need more than "make it better." I need Jesus.

So she risks. She sneaks through the crowd, she reaches out, she settles for the smallest sweep of her fingers along the edge of what was most likely his prayer shawl. It is the least contact that she believes she can have and still be healed.

She is healed. Immediately. The hemorrhaging stops. She's physically fully healed. Her response is to be satisfied with just this minimum amount of contact to obtain healing, and to fade back, unnoticed, into the crowd. She got what she came for, and that's it. No more.

I'm reminded of the many times my young children have tried to sneak a snack right before dinner. They're hungry. They just want the hunger to stop. They want the immediate need fixed. So, Jayna (somehow it always seems to be Jayna!) tiptoes into the pantry and very quietly and unobtrusively pulls out a bag of chips. Then she opens it ever so gently and begins to nibble. And chips satisfy her hunger for a moment, but they don't cure the real hunger within. They don't nourish her deep inside, and they spoil her dinner.

Meanwhile, I'm preparing a full meal for her complete with foods that satisfy: meats, cheese, bread, milk, vegetables, fruit, everything that a body needs to be healthy and happy. I'm setting the table so we can sit around it as a family and share life and relationship. I'm not just planning an empty experience that satisfies the minimum need but, as a loving parent, I'm wanting and preparing to give more, to give a healthy, whole, fully satisfying eating experience.

Just like the woman, when we fall at Jesus's feet and tell him the whole truth— no excuses, no onlys, no ifs, no justs: the whole truth—then he can make us not only healed, but whole.

Jayna would settle for a bag of chips. I want to give her a whole dinner sitting around a table, enjoying one another and the meal. As C. S. Lewis says in *The Weight of Glory*, "It would seem that Our Lord finds our desires not too strong, but too weak . . . like an ignorant child who wants to go on making mud pies in a slum because he cannot imagine what is meant by the offer of a holiday at the sea. We are far too easily pleased."

So why do we settle for a bag of chips when God is preparing a full meal? Do we think we are more likely to receive when we minimize our request? *Just heal me, Lord, and I won't ask for anything more. I'll settle for the minimum.* I think that way sometimes. The bleeding woman thought that way too: "If I can *just* touch his clothes, I'll be healed" (Mark 5:28, emphasis mine). And she is. She's healed. And afterward she wants to disappear back to her old life.

But this isn't what God wants. He's not satisfied with the minimum fix that allows us only to go back to what we've known. He is determined to give us a real meal. What he wants for us is something more, something new, something wondrous. An actual encounter with the living God!

He will settle for nothing less. For her, or for us.

Not Enough for Jesus

Instead of letting us slip away with just the minimum, Jesus will stop the whole crowd. A twelve-year-old girl is dying, a frantic synagogue leader and father is hurrying along hoping they will not be too late, half a town is pressing all around, but Jesus stops anyway. He doesn't stop to heal. He stops to encounter a woman who has already received everything she came for. He stops to call her daughter.

His disciples think he's crazy. "You see the people crowding against you," they say, "and yet you can ask, 'Who touched me?'" (Mark 5:31). It does seem crazy. With a daughter dying, it would seem as if Jesus has better things to do than stop a crowd to find a woman who's already been healed. Why would he bother? What does he hope to gain?

Or perhaps the better question is "What does he hope to give?"

It must be important because Jesus does not stop looking around until the woman steps forward, until she chooses to encounter him despite her fear. Like Jairus, she falls at his feet. But unlike Jairus, she does not come forward in supplication. She is already healed.

Instead, she comes trembling with fear. Sometimes, the "more" that God offers is frightening. We don't know what he'll say. We don't know what he'll do. Will he be disappointed in us? Will he point out our sin in front of the whole town? Will he scold us for daring to come near?

He won't. He doesn't.

Just like the woman, when we fall at Jesus's feet and tell him the whole truth—no excuses, no onlys, no ifs, no justs: the *whole* truth—then he can make us not only healed, but whole.

What Jesus longs for is not so much to stop the bleeding, in her or in us, as it is to look us in the eye and call us "daughter," call us "son." The results of the woman's bleeding would have been not solely physical but relational as well. For twelve years, she was unclean. She would have been ostracized from her community and her family. And worse, she would have been unable to have children and create a family of her own.

Jesus did not normally call those he healed "daughter." In fact, this is the only time Jesus calls someone daughter in all of the Gospels. So why does he choose this intimate, familial word here? I believe it's because in that single word he creates for her a family, he brings her into the family of God. He establishes a close, cherished relationship with this woman whose bleeding lost her any family she would have had. She had no one to claim her as family. She had no one to cherish her. So Jesus names her "daughter." It is her only name in the text, and with it comes a relationship that includes protection, love, and the guarantee of a future, just as any father of that time was expected to care for and protect his daughter and arrange a good marriage for her. A daughter counted on her father to provide whatever she needed to live and procure a bright future with a husband

and children of her own. In the single word *daughter*, Jesus is giving her more than just healing, more than she dared to hope for, more than her faith had won.

Matthew also adds the words "take heart" to Jesus's conversation with the woman. Take heart. Be encouraged. Despair no longer. Do not be afraid. To the weary soul, these words are like water in the desert, like a cool drink after twelve years of nothing but dust.

Jesus is not only restoring her position in a family, his family, he is also restoring her from the hopelessness of years of failure and despair. He is rescuing her from inner weariness.

We reach for so little. We think if we just brush our fingertips against the edge of his clothes we'll have enough, we'll be healed, we'll slip back into the crowd and go about life as it used to be.

But Jesus doesn't work like that. He won't. "It is not enough to simply give her healing," says writer/singer Michael Card. "No, he wants to give her himself."[1]

Take heart. Be encouraged. Despair no longer. Do not be afraid. To the weary soul, these words are like water in the desert, like a cool drink after twelve years of nothing but dust.

She came with her "justs" and "onlys." Just a touch. Only the edge of his cloak. Just stop the bleeding. Only a physical fix. But Jesus is vehemently dissatisfied with all the "justs" and "onlys." Both in the woman's life, and in ours.

He is not the God of Just-the-Minimum. He is not the God of Only. He is never the God of Good Enough.

Who Is This God?

So who is this God?

He is the God of Face-to-Face Hope. He is the God of Unexpected Blessing.

He always has been.

When we are weary, when we are terrified and feel trapped, when we've sent all our resources away in hopes of buying what we long for, when we are alone, that is the time to be like Jacob on the edge of the Jabbok River (Genesis 32).

In Genesis 32, Jacob was afraid that his brother was coming to kill him and take or destroy everything he had. He feared not only the loss of his life, but the loss of his possessions and family as well. He feared what the bleeding woman experienced.

So in the middle of the night, Jacob took all of his family and possessions to the other side of the river. Then he was alone. But he was not alone. Verses 24-30 tell us:

> But Jacob stayed apart by himself, and a man wrestled with him until dawn broke. . . . The man said, "Let me go because the dawn is breaking." But Jacob said, "I won't let you go until you bless me." He said to Jacob, "What's your name?" and he said, "Jacob." Then he said, "Your name won't be Jacob any longer, but Israel, because you struggled with God and with men and won." . . . And he blessed Jacob there. Jacob named the place Peniel, "because I've seen God face-to-face, and my life has been saved."

For Jacob there was never any "good enough." He wouldn't settle for less than a full blessing. He wrestled for it, and would not walk away. For him, there were no "justs" and "onlys." He wanted the most that God would give. He often sought blessing deceitfully, but there was something in him that God prized, because God cannot be manipulated, and yet Jacob did get the blessings.

What are we asking God for? Is it enough? Is it relational? Are we asking to see his face, to know him better, to be a beloved daughter or son?

In our weariness, in our desperation, when we've spent all and done all and have nothing left but one last chance to grab the edge of his garment, remember, there is no sneaking away into the crowd. Our God insists on giving us more than just a healing, only making it stop. He insists on the face-to-face encounter that will heal more than our bodies. It will heal our souls.

Lord, help me not to settle for "good enough"
when I'm tired and broken and out of options.
May I see you for who you really are—a God who loves me
and longs to look into my face so that I might hear the words,
"Take heart, daughter; take heart, son," and be more than healed.
May I always believe that knowing you more deeply
is better than just making the pain stop.
Turn around, Lord. May I see your face today.
May I hear your voice speaking life in my weariness.

"Your daughter has died. Why bother the teacher any longer?"

But Jesus overheard their report and said to the synagogue leader, "Don't be afraid; just keep trusting."

Mark 5:35-36

SEE ALSO MARK 5:21-24, 35-42; MATTHEW 9; LUKE 8.

7

Reaching Through Despair

A Dead Daughter

Why is it that faith is often met with delay? Why do our prayers sometimes result in things just getting worse? How is it that when we come to God in time, in faith and in supplication, sometimes what we love most dies anyway?

Why does Jesus say he's coming but then stop on the road? "Hope delayed makes the heart sick," says Proverbs 13:12. And for Jairus, hope was delayed so long that his only daughter died. Who is this God who dallies, turns around, works in the lives of others, and meanwhile, death comes? Who is this God when it seems too late? Who is he when our hearts cry, "Why bother the teacher any longer?"

Why bother?

Insidious words. Hopeless. The words of despair.

Why bother. Often the words aren't even a question. They're just a dull statement telling us that it's just too late, God didn't act in time, and now there's nothing to do but give up and turn away from the One whom we'd trusted to help.

> *And he taught me that not every delay*
> *ends in death. Sometimes it is good*
> *to wait.*

I've heard those words whispering in my mind. I've felt their weight in my soul. But for Jairus, Jesus didn't let those words linger. He spoke to the hopeless, hurting heart of a father who'd just lost his only child. He invited the man to still believe.

I wonder if it might have happened like this:

~ A Father Tells His Story ~

She wasn't dead when I knelt before him. She wasn't dead when the breeze off the Sea of Galilee rustled my prayer shawl and whispered through the crowd. She wasn't dead when I looked into his face and pleaded for her life. "My little daughter is dying," I cried. "Please come and put your hands on her so that she will be healed and live." And he came.

Was she dead when the dust billowed beneath our feet? Was she dead when the crowd pressed around us? Or did she die only when he delayed? When he stopped, turned, and waited?

I don't know.

All I know is that people came from my house moments ago. They edged through the silent throng. One touched my shoulder. My gaze slipped from Jesus and settled on them. Their words still ring in my ears. "Your daughter is dead."

My only daughter, my beautiful twelve-year-old treasure. Dead.

"Why bother the teacher anymore?"

I shake with the impact of the question. *Why bother?*

Why bother with anything anymore? Why bother to hope? Why bother to pray? Why bother to trust in a wandering rabbi who didn't reach her in time?

I came to him in faith and in hope and in love. I, a synagogue leader, trusted him. He was my only chance.

And now . . . now.

Now it is too late.

Why did he delay?

And why did I bother?

Then he turns to me, this Jesus who disappointed me, who didn't come in time, who paused in the street while my daughter was dying. And now she's dead. He takes a step closer and I see the peace in his eyes.

Peace? Now?

"Don't be afraid." His voice is quiet, spoken not to my ears, but to my broken heart. "Just believe" (NIV).

How can he say that? How can he call me to still hope, still believe, when my daughter is already dead?

And yet he does.

He waited, he delayed. And now he asks the same of me. He asks me to not believe in "too late." He asks me to decide:

Why bother?

Just believe.

Which shall I choose?

I nod at him. For this moment, for a little while, I will delay. I will wait to die inside. I will wait to weep. I will see what he will do.

We walk to my house, at least I assume we do because suddenly it is there before me. I hear the wails of the mourners, the cries of people I know and people I don't. Their voices clatter around me, seem out of place. I want them silenced. They do not help me to wait, to believe.

Jesus turns back to the crowd. He dismisses them with a few words. He won't let them follow him. Instead, he motions to three of his followers. Simon, called Peter now, and the brothers, James and John. Then his gaze flickers to me.

I follow him to the house. He opens the door and the wailing fills my ears. So much noise and chaos and commotion.

I am inside the door now, but I cannot focus. I try to remember to believe. I try to remember to not be afraid. But the howling, the moaning, the keening sobs that ring false in my soul, smother my thoughts.

Then, in the midst of the cacophony, his voice speaks. "Why all this commotion and wailing? The child is not dead but asleep."

They laugh at him.

I do not laugh.

Do not be afraid. Just believe . . .

So I believe.

He sends them out, all of them. All the mockers, all the weepers, all the wailers. They are gone. And in their place is a waiting silence. A silence that beckons me to not yet despair.

My gaze catches that of my wife. Her face is stark, her eyes red and puffy. But she doesn't cry now. Instead she just looks at me with confusion. Why did I bring the teacher when it was already too late? I see the question in her eyes. But I have no answer. I walk over and take her hand in mine. We do not speak. We cannot.

Jesus glances at my wife with a look so full of compassion that I can barely breathe. She pauses for a moment. Then she looks to the other room.

Jesus nods once and beckons us to follow. I start to tremble as his disciples and my wife follow him. I know where they're going. To her body. Can I endure seeing the body of . . . of . . .

Don't be afraid. Just believe.

I swallow, square my shoulders, and allow my feet to take me where I don't want to go.

When I enter the room, he is kneeling beside her. She is pale and there is no breath. He takes her by the hand and his voice whispers through the room. "Talitha koum!" He tells my little girl to get up.

And she does.

She does!

I gasp. We all do. Except for her. She walks around the room.

For a moment I am frozen to the spot. Her mother is not. She rushes forward, holds my living, breathing, walking, and no-longer-pale daughter in her arms.

"Don't tell anyone about this," I hear Jesus say. And then I am with them, my family, whole, healed, and filled with awe.

Jesus comes near us. He smiles. "Give her something to eat."

To eat, of course. Because she is no walking ghost. She is not an apparition. She is alive, truly, fully alive. And she needs to eat.

I almost laugh. When it was too late for healing, when all that made sense was "why bother," this rabbi, this strange teacher from the shore, did more than heal. He raised my daughter, he raised my hope, my faith, my life, from the dead. He did not heal. He resurrected.

And he taught me that not every delay ends in death. Sometimes it is good to wait.

Reaching for Wonder

I've written a whole book on learning to wait well. I wrote it because I'm terrible at waiting, and every single thing I've learned about doing it well has been learned the hard way. It's been learned the way Jairus learned, through what seemed like unnecessary pain, through God's delays, through deaths and resurrections.

> *Sometimes God delays. Sometimes he allows death to come even when we've had faith, we've prayed, we've come to him in time. And in the delay, before the promises, before resurrection, before we know what will happen next, he asks us to "just believe."*

The problem is, death is hard. A subsequent resurrection doesn't make the pain of hearing "your daughter's dead" any easier. It hurts. It chokes. It tears through our very souls.

Wouldn't it be better if God came sooner, before the excruciating grief? Wouldn't it be better if Jesus arrived before the daughter died? If he walked faster, started sooner, didn't stop and turn away to talk to the bleeding woman? Or wouldn't it have been better if Jesus had healed Jairus's daughter from afar as he did for others in the Gospels?

But he didn't. He could have. But Jesus let that girl die.

Apparently, our happiness is not so high on Jesus's list of priorities. If it were, he would never delay. He wouldn't tell us "don't be afraid, just believe," because he would work before we had reason to fear.

The purpose of the pause, then, is not to hurt us. It's not to push us to despair. Rather, it's to ask us to grow deeper, trust more, to wait and to watch what he will do when it seems that there's nothing left to do, when it seems like it's too late.

But sometimes God delays. Sometimes he allows death to come even when we've had faith, we've prayed, we've come to him in time. And in the delay, before the promises, before resurrection, before we know what will happen next, he asks us to "just believe."

When God Delays

Jairus does nothing wrong. As soon as Jesus comes back from across the Sea of Galilee, Jairus approaches him. He doesn't wait until the last minute. He doesn't exhaust all other options. He doesn't hang back but comes directly to Jesus with his need. Then, as soon as he sees Jesus, he falls at Jesus's feet in a posture of reverence and humility. This is no arrogant asking. Mark 5:22-24 tells us, "Jairus, one of the synagogue leaders, came forward. When he saw Jesus, he fell at his feet and pleaded with him, 'My daughter is about to die. Please, come and place your hands on her so that she can be healed and live.' So Jesus went with him." Jairus doesn't bargain with Jesus. He doesn't call upon his status as a synagogue leader to imply that he deserves Jesus's help. He simply asks in faith for Jesus to come and lay hands on his daughter so she might live.

And Jesus comes.

All seems well. Everything is going just as it should when a person comes to Jesus with an urgent request spoken with humble faith.

And then Jesus stops.

He turns around.

The woman he stops to find has already been healed. No delay seems necessary. And yet Jesus stops anyway.

In the interval, in the time it takes for Jesus to stop walking toward Jairus's house, the unthinkable happens. News comes that it is too late. Jesus is too late. Jairus's daughter has died.

The messengers urge Jairus to not bother the teacher anymore. The request for healing didn't go as hoped or planned. The girl died anyway. Despite Jairus's faith, despite Jesus going with him, his daughter is dead . . . just as if he had never asked at all.

And yet Jesus is not dismayed. He's not wringing his hands. He's not offering apologies to a father who had counted on him for a healing. Scholar David Garland says, "Jesus is not thrown off guard by this dismal news of the girl's demise. His concern is for the continued faith of the father. Jairus was confident that Jesus could heal his daughter, but he did not bargain for this."[1]

We never bargain for the delay that leads to death. Why delay? Why wait until death? What does this accomplish? Why doesn't Jesus come in time to spare us grief? In the face of these questions, in the face of a God whose timing doesn't always make sense to us, Jesus doesn't apologize and he doesn't scold. Instead he calls us to deeper faith, a deeper belief, right at the time when we are reeling. Just when it seems that God hasn't done what we trusted him to do, he says to us, as he said to Jairus, "Don't be afraid; just keep trusting" (v. 36).

The purpose of the pause, then, is not to hurt us. It's not to push us to despair. Rather, it's to ask us to grow deeper, trust more, to wait and to watch what he will do when it seems that there's nothing left to do, when it seems like it's too late.

And in that moment, we are faced with a choice between faith and "why bother."

Why Bother?

When coming to God with our needs doesn't work out the way we'd hoped, the temptation is to give up and to give in, not to anger or sorrow, but to despair. When I talk to marriage counselors, they tell me that when a couple is angry with each other, there's hope. When they seem to hate each other, there's hope. When there's fight and fury, when there's sorrow and tears, there's still hope. When we feel, we can be reconciled.

He asks us to just believe when there is no longer any earthly reason to believe at all.

Indifference, however, is an enemy that is most difficult to overcome. It's when we just don't care anymore, when death leads to despair, when we don't stomp away but we shuffle . . . that's the real enemy to hope and faith, to belief. It's the kind of despair that, in the face of the seemingly purposeless delay, simply says, "Why bother?"

Those are exactly the words that Jairus confronted when he found out his daughter was dead. "Why bother the teacher any longer?" the messengers said. Why not just leave Jesus in the street and forget about faith? After all, Jesus didn't act in time. He didn't come as soon as needed. He didn't do what he was counted on to do. Instead, the daughter died. Despite Jairus doing everything right, his daughter died anyway.

So why bother?

For Jairus, and for us, this kind of death is a crossroads. At the exact place and time when Jesus has most disappointed us, most let us down, when we are the most shaken by our worst fears come true, Jesus asks us to choose between "why bother" and "just believe." Mark 5:36 says, "But Jesus overheard [the messengers'] report and said to the synagogue leader, 'Don't be afraid; just keep trusting.'"

At the very moment when belief seems the most ridiculous, when walking away seems the most rational thing to do, Jesus asks us to wait, to not give up yet, to keep trusting when it is clearly too late. He asks us to just believe when there is no longer any earthly reason to believe at all.

It is not an easy choice. Just like Jairus, we come face-to-face with barriers to faith. And not just one, but many. Jairus overcomes the first barrier of "why bother." He doesn't walk away. Instead he goes with Jesus to his house. He wants Jesus to come even though his daughter is already dead, even though it doesn't seem like there's anything Jesus can do to help now.

But when he arrives at his home, more obstacles to faith meet him. Mourners, weeping and wailing, assault his ears. Jesus takes charge. He enters the house and says, "What's all this commotion and crying about? The child isn't dead. She's only sleeping" (v. 39).

And again, Jairus is faced with a choice to despair or to just keep trusting. The mourners laugh at Jesus. They know it is too late. We, too, hear the mourners laugh.

When deaths come into our lives, when all seems lost, done, over, sealed and buried, dead and gone, Jesus doesn't heal, he resurrects.

Sometimes, faith in the face of death seems laughable. It's crazy. Healing is one thing, but now it's too late to believe anymore. Jairus had faith, he went to the shore, he called on Jesus, but the girl died. Now it's time for mourning. Now it's time for despair. Or is it?

David Garland comments, "The mourners here create an obstacle to Jairus's faith. He must now ignore them and trust that Jesus can do the impossible by bringing his little girl back to life."[2]

It makes so much sense to stay outside with the mourners. It makes sense to give up and accept that what's done is done.

But what if we don't? Mark 5:40 says, "[The mourners] laughed at [Jesus], but he threw them all out." Jesus has no time for the naysayers. We shouldn't either. What if, in the face of too-late, we walk past the mourners; what if we follow Jesus into the back room? What if we can face our dead daughters with Jesus instead of hanging with the mockers and the "don't bother-ers"? What if we choose to not despair and instead simply face our grief by following Jesus to the house, into the house, past the mourners who mock, into the very room that holds the thing we fear most to see?

If we can wait to be overwhelmed, if we can walk past the mourners and the mockers, if we can allow Jesus to "throw them all out," then we may just discover, with Jairus, the surprising wonder of "too late."

The Wonder of Too Late

The story of Jairus tells us that it's never too late with God. When deaths come into our lives, when all seems lost, done, over, sealed and buried, dead and gone, Jesus doesn't heal, he resurrects.

We want God to heal before the hurt grows worse. But sometimes, he is aiming for the bigger miracle. Sometimes he doesn't want to make it better, he wants to make it new.

Might it be possible that Jesus is not too late but we are simply still on the road to home?

I wrestle with this idea, this truth, and I find that I don't like it. I want God to heal, to make it better, before I have to face the despair of death, before I have to choose between "why bother" and "just believe." I wrestle as I think of my six miscarriages, each baby prayed for desperately before death came. I wrestle as I remember the heartfelt prayers of a six-year-old before her pony died of cancer. I wrestle as I watch my friend whose husband left her after a decades-long marriage, despite all her prayers and hopes. I wrestle as I read posts about kids who die from diabetes and pray for a cure that, if it comes, will come too late for those families who grieve.

Too late. Where is this so-called wonder of "too late" in the face of such grief? Not everyone's daughter gets raised from the dead. Not everyone's heartache is erased in a single moment.

And yet . . . and yet . . . does God ever delay without purpose? Does he ever shrug his shoulders and walk away without care? I don't believe so. And I wonder if maybe, in the things that break our hearts, we judge too soon. Might it be possible that Jesus is not too late but we are simply still on the road to home? Still in the yard while the mourners wail? Maybe Jesus has just not yet taken our dead hopes by the hand.

Maybe we are in the dark day between death and resurrection. Maybe the dawn is coming with an unexpected resurrection.

Who Is This God?

After all, our God is the God of Resurrection. In the days before Jesus died, there were many opportunities for him to save himself. He prayed in time. In the garden of Gethsemane he prayed with fervor and faith. And yet they came to arrest him anyway.

He could have fought them in the garden. Instead, he healed the ear of the servant of the high priest who had come with the group to arrest him. When he was taken before Pilate, he could have argued for his release. When he was taken to Herod, he could have performed a miracle and been freed. When he stood before the crowds, he could have pleaded for justice. Pilate argued in his defense, but Jesus stayed silent.

Arrest led not to freedom but to beating, mocking, and the sentence of death.

Even then it was not too late. "Save yourself!" the people cried, mocking him, as he hung on the cross. But he didn't call down angels to save him. Instead, he died.

He let the worst happen. What all his followers feared most came to be. And then they took his dead body off the cross, and still he didn't come back to life. They wrapped his body, they buried him, they sealed the tomb. And days passed.

And it is the same for the deaths in our lives. Jesus means to defeat death, to resurrect the beauty, the wonder, in our lives, not to simply let us avoid the pain. Jesus intends us to experience the cross before we encounter the empty tomb.

When everyone was sure it was all over, it was too late, only then did the stone roll away. Then the angels spoke. Then he appeared to followers who didn't understand that he needed to defeat death, not just avoid it. He needed to go through it, not around it. He needed to resurrect, not just to be healed.

He needed to die.

And it is the same for the deaths in our lives. Jesus means to defeat death, to resurrect the beauty, the wonder, in our lives, not to simply let us avoid the pain.

Jesus intends us to experience the cross before we encounter the empty tomb.

Lord, when it seems too late, when I'm afraid you didn't come in time,
when I am tempted to say "why bother" and walk away,
remind me that you are the God of Resurrection,
and resurrection is even better
than healing. Whisper to my soul, "Don't be afraid, just believe,"
and give me the strength to walk past the mourners
and follow you into the room I dread to enter.
Help me to trust you enough to face the things I fear most.

When Jesus saw him lying there, knowing that he had already been there a long time, he asked him, "Do you want to get well?"

The sick man answered him, "Sir, I don't have anyone who can put me in the water when it is stirred up. When I'm trying to get to it, someone else has gotten in ahead of me."

John 5:6-7

SEE ALSO JOHN 5:1-18.

8

Reaching Through Excuses

Do You Want to Be Well?

D o you want to get well?

Seems like a simple enough question, especially if you've been sick for decades. The answer is yes! Of course it's yes. How could it be anything else?

And yet it is. Sometimes, it's something else entirely.

In the story of the man who had been sick for thirty-eight years, and in my own story, there are places where the answer is not a resounding yes. There are places where I answer with excuses. Reasons why healing is impossible. Explanations about why I'm still stuck. Clarifications, elucidations, justifications, rationalizations. And not a simple "Yes, I want to get well" for any of it.

When we've been stuck in a bad place for so long that we forget what "well" looks like, God doesn't approach us with justifications and rationalizations. He comes with a simple question that pierces through all the excuses.

Do you actually, truly, want to get well?

That's all that matters.

God doesn't need a list of potential obstacles. He doesn't require us to point out why we have to stay sick. He just asks if we're willing to be well.

Too often when we live with sickness for so long, it becomes a sickness of the soul. We no longer hope for healing. Instead, we settle into our condition and blame others for it.

Apparently, that is the most important question of all.

For the man who was sick for nearly four decades, it might have happened like this:

A Sick Man Tells His Story

A sheep gate. Jerusalem's north wall. A festival. Five covered porticoes. And a pool. A pool that heals through angels' wings.

None of that matters.

What matters is the crush of bodies surrounding the pool. Sick, blind, lame, paralyzed. People like me. Faster than me. Someone always gets to the pool first when the water is troubled. Someone else always has help. *No one helps me.*

So I lie here on my mat and turn away from the glint of water being refreshed, renewed. I focus on the stench of sick bodies. Thirty-eight years. I barely smell them anymore. I rattle my cup filled with coins. Someone coughs. Another groans. Thirty-eight years. I barely hear them anymore.

I wouldn't come here except it's a good place to beg. I start here. Then I go to the temple. It is the same every day. I've become very good at being pitiable in these past decades. The pool draws the guilty-in-spirit as much as it draws the sick. But the temple is better. They go in feeling guilty, they go out feeling the same, and that means more coins in my money bag.

"Poor man," someone says and drops a coin. I don't even look up.

Others gather closer to the water. They believe it heals. Maybe it does. Maybe it doesn't. Some have been healed. I've never been first, so I wouldn't know. And I don't care. Not anymore.

A stranger approaches. Quickly, I sneak coins from the cup into my money bag. I can't have too many or he will give to another. I can't have none or he will think I am not in need. I know well the ins and outs of the begging game. I am good at it. I have to be.

The man draws closer. A few others follow him. He steps up to my mat, but he does not drop a coin.

I wait.

Then I look up.

He holds no money, but he is staring into my eyes as if trying to see my thoughts. My fingers inch toward the cup, but his words stop me.

They stop me cold.

"Do you want to get well?"

What strange question is this? Do I want to be well? Of course I do. Don't I? Everyone here does. Why should he offend me with his ridiculous query? Why doesn't he just drop some money into my cup and be gone, like everyone else? Do I want to be well? It's almost an accusation, as if I lie here because I choose it. As if it's my own fault.

I huff. I puff. I scowl. I frown. "Sir," the words come out of me like clippings of chaff. "I don't have anyone who can put me in the water when it is stirred up. When I'm trying to get to it, someone else has gotten in ahead of me."

It's the truth. Sort of. It's not my fault I am lame and sick and lying here begging. It's not my fault. No one helps me. I don't have any choice. How dare this stranger imply otherwise.

"Get up!"

His voice isn't questioning anymore. It's commanding. Something in me pushes to obey. Then, I feel the strength.

"Pick up your mat and walk."

I get up. I pick up my mat. I walk. I can't help it.

I walk through the crowd. I walk toward the temple. I walk.

With my mat. On a Sabbath.

I don't think of that until the religious leaders stop on their way to the temple and approach me. They frown. Do they not recognize me now that I am on my feet and not at theirs? Perhaps they've never seen me at all. Until now.

Their scowls deepen. "It's the Sabbath!" one says. "You aren't allowed to carry your mat," growls another.

They're blaming me! But it's not my fault. I didn't do anything wrong. I'm not the Sabbath-breaker. The man who healed me is. They need to understand that. "The man who made me well said to me, 'Pick up your mat and walk.'"

"Who is this man who said to you, 'Pick it up and walk'?"

I shrug, glad that they've shifted the blame to him. I don't know who the man was. He slipped off into the crowd after he healed me.

He healed me.

Now what am I going to do?

I meander toward the temple. I glance behind me. The religious leaders still watch me, then the crowd blocks me from their view.

I follow the path that I do every day. Toward the temple, money bag attached at my waist, cup tucked in my mat. All I know is how to beg. It will be harder now. I hunch over a little.

I try walking with a limp. I dig out the cup, hold it up, and try a little groan.

Someone drops in a coin.

I enter the temple. A man steps in front of me. I look up. My healer stands with his face stern.

I swallow and tuck the cup away. But he's seen it. I know he has.

He leans toward me, his gaze catching mine. Holding it. "See! You have been made well. Don't sin anymore in case something worse happens to you."

Sin? I'm not to blame. How can he tell me to stop sinning? I clench my jaw, turn, and see the religious leaders coming toward the temple. I didn't know who healed me before. But I know now. He's the one who caused me to sin on the Sabbath, and he dares to lecture me in the temple.

Just because he healed me doesn't mean he can treat me like that. I should have known when he asked me if I wanted to be healed. Ridiculous, condescending question.

I want to be healed.

Just not like this.

Reaching for Wonder

You would think that after decades of suffering, anyone would want to be healed by any means. But often, that's not how it works. Somewhere in the years of his sickness, the man at the pool stopped looking for healing and started focusing on excuses.

When our response to God in our long disease, pain, sickness, or hurt is about blame and not about our need, something's gone wrong.

So when Jesus asks him a simple question, "Do you want to get well?" the man has no simple answer. Instead, he gives an excuse as to why he hasn't yet been healed. He answers with the reason he believes he must stay stuck in his condition.

How discouraging! And yet, how perfectly normal. Too often when we live with sickness for so long, it becomes a sickness of the soul. We no longer hope for healing. Instead, we settle into our condition and blame others for it, just like the man by the pool.

He is more focused on how others haven't helped him than he is on the real question: "Do you want to get well?" The man never answers that question at all. Instead, he answers other, imagined, questions—"Why aren't you well? Why are you still sick?"

And his answer to these questions is essentially, "It's not my fault!"

When our response to God in our long disease, pain, sickness, or hurt is about blame and not about our need, something's gone wrong.

Something's gone terribly, terribly wrong.

129

It's Their Fault

In the face of the question that should be the easiest question of his life, this man chooses not healing but finger-pointing. "There is no one," he says. To him, the only answer is the pool, and others have not done their part to get him to the pool in a timely enough manner for him to be healed. It never even occurs to him that he might find healing in another way.

The belief at the time was that when angels stirred the water of the pool, the first person to enter the pool afterward would be healed. He couldn't get to the pool quickly enough. No one helped him. Therefore, in his mind, he was stuck. There was only one way to be well, and no one made that way possible for him.

In other words, it was their fault he remained sick and lame. It wasn't his fault. And that's all that mattered, even in the face of a question meant to engender new hope.

Michael Card writes, "Jesus's question, 'Do you want to get well?' points to the fact that the lack of strength in the man's body was nothing compared to the weakness of his will."[1]

With his Messiah and Savior standing before him, the one who can heal him, the one who asks if he wants this healing, this man can only think of excuses and who's to blame.

And that, more than any decades of physical illness, is enough to break my heart. How often does Jesus come to me and offer a miracle and all I can say is, "It's not my fault"?

It's Not My Fault

And yet, in response to me, to the man at the pool, Jesus doesn't talk about blame at all. He sticks with his simple question: Do you *want* to be healed? Not, can you be healed, or should you be healed, or even do you have the faith to be healed. He just asks what we really want, what is the true desire of our hearts.

Recently, my husband asked that same question to one of his close friends, a friend who is on the brink of divorce, who has lost hope for his marriage, and has settled into the blame game. "Do you *want* your marriage to be healed?"

She doesn't meet my needs.

I don't love her anymore.

It's been too long.

She doesn't want to try.

She doesn't care.

Excuses. Blame. A million reasons why the marriage can't be saved and divorce is the only option. And all the time, God, who blessed their union, is simply asking, "Do you want to be healed?"

What do you really want?

Because Jesus doesn't care about our excuses. He won't play the blame game. Not for you, for me, for my husband's friend, or for the man who lies by a pool and no longer believes in healing.

Jesus offers not a way into a pool, but an encounter with the God who created man to walk.

Jesus doesn't blame others for the man's illness. Nor does he blame the man. There is no "you could have gotten to the pool" or "this mess is your own doing." He just asks whether the man wants healing, true healing, in the right way. No pool, no angels troubling the surface of the water, no myths, no trusting "if I was just quick enough, smart enough, savvy enough." Jesus offers not a way into a pool, but an encounter with the God who created man to walk.

No More Excuses

And perhaps that is why Jesus, in the face of the man's excuses, heals him anyway. The man never says he wants it, he never asks in the right way, in fact, he never asks at all. And still Jesus heals. Why? I think it's because there are no excuses that are good enough to thwart God's intent in our lives. Even our lack of faith, even our discouragement, fears, being stuck so long we can't imagine anything else, cannot thwart God. While we use excuses to explain our long sickness, why we can't be healed, why we have to be stuck where we've always been, Jesus uses his power and purpose to make moot all and any excuses we can dream up.

The man couldn't imagine being free, but Jesus freed him anyway.

And there were no more excuses.

I'm reminded of a man I recently met at a Community Alliance for Safety and Peace meeting in my city. I sat in my chair facing the center of a ring of tables as one by one community nonprofit leaders introduced themselves and their organizations. I heard about people working in the schools to stop bullying. I listened to a man talk about his work with foster kids. I smiled as a group told of their progress with promoting peace and hope for gang members. And then a small man stood. His skin was covered with tattoos; they crawled up his neck and peppered the sides of his face. Gang tattoos.

He straightened his shoulders. "I'm so glad to be with you," he said. And then he told his story of being in prison, often in solitary confinement, for twenty-seven years. He told of his life sentence, ended suddenly not by death but by prison over-crowding. He made no excuses. He placed no blame.

Instead he talked about what he was doing with his unexpected freedom. He had partnered with a church and was now working with gang-impacted youth to free them from gangs and keep them from following his path to prison. He had gotten back his life, and now he was giving it away.

There were so many excuses he could have used to stay stuck. He'd been nearly three decades in prison and it was all he knew. He had committed horrible crimes. The gang was his identity. No one had taken him to the pool when the angel stirred the water.

But in those few minutes in which he spoke, there was not even a hint of blame or of bitterness. All he talked about was changing lives. All that mattered was that he'd been given a chance to be healed.

No excuses, not for anyone. No matter the past, Jesus can heal. Jesus can set free. Just not always in the way we expect.

Fully Healed?

The question is, do we really *want* this kind of healing, this kind of freedom? Because simply removing excuses does not necessarily heal the soul. The man by the pool was healed in body, but he never did submit to Jesus in faith. He got up, he wandered around, but he didn't know who Jesus was. Unlike the woman with the issue of blood, this man never looked Jesus in the face and allowed him to heal him on the inside as well as the outside. He took the healing, but rejected the relationship.

When the Jewish leaders asked, "Who is this man who said to you, 'Pick it up and walk'?" (v. 12), the man had no idea who Jesus was. And when Jesus found him again in the temple, there were no words of gratitude, no falling on his knees in thanksgiving or reverence. He doesn't say a word to Jesus.

It's not about blame. It's never about blame. It's not about excuses for staying stuck. It's about the purpose of the threshing: to make something new, something useful, something good.

But Jesus says something to him: "See! You have been made well. Don't sin anymore in case something worse happens to you" (v. 14). Ouch! Those are harsh words. How starkly they stand in contrast to Jesus's words to the woman healed after twelve years of bleeding. To her he said, "Daughter, your faith has healed you; go in peace, healed from your disease" (Mark 5:34). But to this man, there is no "my son," there is no commendation of faith, there is no blessing as he leaves. Something is still not right in this man's heart.

That brokenness of soul is revealed most clearly when the man immediately leaves Jesus's presence and tattles on him to the Jewish leaders. John 5:16 tells us, "As a result, the Jewish leaders were harassing Jesus, since he had done these things on the Sabbath." And a couple verses later we read, "For this reason the Jewish leaders wanted even more to kill him" (v. 18).

Michael Card says,

Here is one who met the Son, felt His power, was even healed by Him, and yet betrays Him. Truly this man is the other Judas of the Scriptures. . . . What is most unbelievable, puzzling, even disturbing, is that the healing was incomplete. The heart of the man Jesus left untouched. As he walked away, it seemed his soul was just as crippled as it was when we first saw him sitting like a sack of potatoes by the pool.[2]

Why? Because as much as it seems that anyone would want to be healed after thirty-eight years, the true answer to Jesus's question was no. No, he did not really want to be healed. No, he didn't want to be free. No, he didn't want his life changed by the God who heals and makes whole.

He had gotten used to his misery. It had become his identity. He was comfortable living with the excuses that assured him that nothing would ever change.

Except it did. And he didn't.

And that is the true tragedy. This man was threshed, but he wouldn't allow himself to become bread.

Who Is This God?

Isaiah 28:28-29 says:

> Bread grain is crushed,
>> but the thresher doesn't thresh it forever.
> He drives the cart wheel over it;
>> he spreads it out but doesn't crush it.
> This also comes from the Lord of heavenly
> forces,
>> who gives wondrous counsel and increases
>> wisdom.

Threshing is "the process of loosening the edible part of cereal grain (or other crop) from the scaly, inedible chaff that surrounds it. It is the step in grain preparation after harvesting and before win-nowing, which separates the loosened chaff from the grain."[3]

Threshing is difficult. Sometimes it takes a long time. Sometimes it feels like a beating, as if the cattle have been stomping you for-ever or the threshing wheel crushing you over and over and over. And yet, Isaiah assures us that the threshing will not go on forever, because threshing is for a purpose. It's to get rid of the chaff. It is to prepare the grain for making bread.

It's not about blame. It's never about blame. It's not about excuses for staying stuck. It's about the purpose of the threshing: to make something new, something useful, something good.

Psalm 104:14-15 says of God:

> You make grass grow for cattle;
> > you make plants for human farming
> > > in order to get food from the ground,
> > > and wine, which cheers people's hearts,
> > > along with oil, which makes the face shine,
> > > and bread, which sustains the human heart.

Our God is the God of Bread-Making. He doesn't thresh us forever. Instead, he makes us into bread to bless and sustain others.

We can only be all we need to be in Christ when we accept the God of Bread-Making. It's not about who's to blame for what hap-pened before. It's not about who's to blame for what might come. It's about what God is doing right before us, right now. It's about him asking the question, "Do you want to get well?"

Do you want to be made into bread?

Lord, no excuses, no blame, no reasons why I have to be stuck.
I come to you to say, "Yes! I want to be healed!"
I really, truly, fully want to be well in every part of me.
Cleanse me from complacency,
thresh me until I am ready to be made into bread.
Find me by the pool and make me whole.

"The children have to be fed first. It isn't right to take the children's bread and toss it to the dogs." But she answered, "Lord, even the dogs under the table eat the children's crumbs."

Mark 7:27-28

See also Mark 7:24-30; Matthew 15:21-28.

9

REACHING THROUGH SCORN

Dogs and a Syrophoenician Mother

Is Jesus rude? Is he condescending? Is he just flat-out mean? It's easy to think, "Of course not!" We naturally want to deny such crazy allegations without a second thought.

And then we come to this story of Jesus and a Syrophoenician mother. We encounter his talk of dogs and children and bread meant for the table. Disturbing images that defy a tidy faith.

So we have a choice. Will we ignore this strange story, will we flip the page and settle on something simpler? Or will we face it? Will we look deeply and let it shake us, trouble us, and make us encounter this God who doesn't always speak as we expect?

Shall we ask the hard questions, seek the deep truths? Shall we trust that it is in the uncomfortable places of our encounters with Christ, in the very places where we feel faith stutter, where suppositions tremble, where beliefs quiver, that we can shake off the shallowness of our faith and stumble deeper than we ever dreamed?

For the Syrophoenician woman, it might have happened like this:

⸺ A Mother Tells Her Story ⸺

A whispered rumor. A hidden hope. He has come.

So I watch the house. I wait. I will wait all day, all night, if I have to. I will wait forever for this chance to free my daughter from the spirit that torments her. I don't care if this Jesus wants to stay concealed. I don't care if he wishes to remain unknown.

I care about my daughter. And I know this man, this rabbi from a country foreign to my own, can heal her.

The sun climbs in the sky. It reaches its zenith. It begins to descend.

And that's when I see him. He exits the house with the men who follow him. My chance has come.

"Show me mercy, Son of David," I cry. "My daughter is suffering terribly from demon possession."

He doesn't look at me; he doesn't even glance my way. But he's seen me. I know he has.

I hurry toward him, crying for mercy.

His men lean in. Between breaths I hear their words. "Send her away; she keeps shouting out after us."

I won't be sent away. Not like this.

I rush closer and fall at his feet. I dare not look up.

He pauses.

I take a breath. "Lord, help me! Throw the demon out of my daughter."

For a moment there is silence.

Then he speaks, quietly, slowly, as if drawing out every word. "It is not good to take the children's bread and toss it to dogs."

Dogs. I have heard this saying before. We who are not Jewish are the dogs. The Jews are the children. And yet he uses a different word than the one typically used for dogs. He changes the saying, replaces *dogs* with the word for puppies, for the small pets we feed from under our tables. It is almost a word of endearment. But . . . I wonder . . .

Is he teasing me?

I dare to glance up.

His eyes look intently into mine, as if . . . as if he is willing me to think more deeply, see what I could not before see. There is an invitation there.

Will I take it?

I will.

A small smile dances across my face. It is matched by his. Confidence flows through me. He has dared me to stand up to the prejudice. He has dared me to defy the narrow-mindedness of nations and peoples. For my daughter, how can I do any less?

I tilt up my chin. "Yes, Lord," I say.

He nods, willing me to continue. He wants me to answer. He wants me to . . . banter? Who is this man, this healer?

I raise my eyebrows and straighten my shoulders. "But even the dogs under the table eat the children's crumbs."

Delight springs into his eyes. And he laughs. He laughs out loud.

"Good answer! Woman, you have great faith." He grins down at me. "The demon has already left your daughter."

I rise to my feet and cock my head at him. Joy emanates from every part of him. It reflects off me. My daughter is healed. She is free.

And yet, I know that her healing is not all that has happened here. It is not the casting away of the demon that delights this man, this rabbi, this Lord in front of me. It is that I saw him, I really saw.

And he saw me.

What looked like an insult was really an invitation in disguise.

Reaching for Wonder

We miss the wonder of this story when we don't see the subtleties of Jesus's wording and approach. We bring our assumptions instead of our souls, and in doing so we miss the depth of what God is offering in this simple, strange encounter.

At this point in Jesus's ministry, he has traveled forty miles up the coast of the Mediterranean into Gentile country. Both Mark and Matthew tell us that this woman was a Gentile, an outsider. Mark calls her "Greek, Syrophoenician by birth." Matthew says, "a Canaanite woman from those territories" (of Tyre and Sidon). Sidon was the city from which the wicked queen Jezebel of Israel's history came (1 Kings 16:31). So our Syrophoenician mother had no heritage, no superior breeding, nothing to claim that would recommend her to Jesus. She was of the wrong race, from the wrong family, living in the wrong region.

Will we settle for just the crumbs? Are they enough? Do they have to be?

It wasn't uncommon for the Jews of the day to call her people dogs, much as people today might call others pigs. According to Leviticus 11:27, dogs (like pigs) were considered unclean under the Law. Therefore, when Gentiles were called dogs, it was a degrading and demeaning term.

So at first glance, Jesus's words seem to be the worst kind of bigotry and insult. First he ignores her, then he scorns her by calling her a dog. What could be worse?

And yet, when we look closer we see an interesting twist. Jesus doesn't use the word for stray dog, unwanted dog, lesser-than dog. Instead, he tweaks the saying by using the term for puppy, or small, pet dog. While not common in the Jewish culture because dogs were unclean, it was very common in the woman's culture, in Tyre and Sidon, the region Jesus was in when he encountered the woman, for families to keep small dogs as pets. These pups were well-loved, cherished, and fed scraps from the family table.

By using this particular term, Jesus is setting a choice before her. Will she be offended and walk away, or will she choose to look deeper and see the opportunity he is offering to her, an opportunity for a unique encounter with the heart of Christ?

Is Jesus Calling Me a Dog?

Jesus offers us that same opportunity. He may not allude that we're dogs, but in our desperation it often feels like he's scorning us through silence. We pray and it seems like he's ignoring us. Others get answers to prayer and we don't, and we feel as if he was sent to others and doesn't care about our pain. We come and fall at his feet, but nothing seems to change. We feel like he's treating us as lesser, beneath, unworthy of his attention.

"It isn't right to take the children's bread and toss it to the dogs." We are not children. We are just dogs.

And so the discouragement, the anger, the frustration and fear bubble to the surface of our souls.

Will we settle for just the crumbs? Are they enough? Do they have to be?

Just like the Syrophoenician mother, we are faced with a choice. Do we hear the invitation in Christ's silence, in his supposed scorn? Or do we simply become indignant and walk away?

The woman couldn't afford to walk away. Her daughter's life was at stake. So she chose the way of love. She chose trust. She chose to engage.

Perhaps because she knew what it meant to be treasured like a pup beneath the table. Perhaps because she was humble enough to know that even a pup is loved.

I remember the day our family got a new little dog to love. Two of my daughters went horseback riding in the wee hours of the morning on the first day of summer vacation. They threw bridles on their horses and rode bareback through the trails and trees at the back of our property. That's where they found a little white-haired dog, dirty, emaciated, trembling with fear.

They dismounted their horses, squatted down, and coaxed him out of the brush. It took some time, but eventually he came, his ratty tail tucked between his legs.

She wants the healing so desperately that she doesn't try to pretend, she just encounters Jesus with everything she is.

Despite his fear and bad experiences with people, he encountered, he engaged. He dared to risk scorn for a chance to be healed.

So of course, my daughters hauled him home. And of course their first words were, "Can we keep him?"

Max was a stray dog, a small dog, a skinny, sickly looking thing. He was not at all the kind of dog we would have chosen or were looking for (boxer fans that we are!).

So of course we kept him. We washed him, fed him, healed him.

We fed him some more. And in time he became the dog he was meant to be.

When he came to us, he was scared and suspicious. He was afraid we would abandon him, scorn him, throw him away. Instead, we called him to a deeper experience. We offered him not just food, but a home, a family, a forever.

That's what God is offering to us. He's calling us not to a quick-fix meal, a quick-fix bath, a quick-fix cure.

He's calling us deeper into the family of God.

An Invitation to Deep Faith

Jesus's encounter with the Syrophoenician woman was also not about the "quick fix" but was an invitation to deeper faith. The disciples (as usual) wanted Jesus to send her away. She was an annoyance. She was a Gentile. She was a woman. But Jesus stopped to talk with this female, Gentile outsider. He could have simply healed the daughter and sent her away, but instead he insisted on this unique encounter. He insisted on the opportunity to invite her to the table.

Instead of simply healing and heading out, Jesus took the time to engage with her, challenge her to take a step. He prodded her where she would be most sensitive, in the area of her race and heritage.

And to her credit, she chose to see Jesus's words as an invitation to a table experience. An invitation to be closer, to be treasured. Because that's what dogs were in her culture and often in ours. They were, and are, often members of the table.

All the Syrophoenician woman wanted was to be near enough to lick up the crumbs. It was enough to be invited to the table.

The contrast between this Gentile woman and the lame man by the pool in Jerusalem is astounding. There we had a Jew, in the center of Judaism, with every right and privilege afforded by his heritage. Jesus encountered him. He was at Jesus's feet, but not because he fell there in humility. It was his sickness that forced him to be where he was. When Jesus asked him a question, he never said he wanted to be healed. He gave excuses. And later when Jesus said, "Stop sinning!" the man left in a prideful huff to tattle to the religious leaders.

The Syrophoenician woman, on the other hand, had no such privilege due to heritage, gender, or background. She chose to fall at the feet of a Jewish rabbi, in humility, and ask for what her heart so desperately desired. She offered no excuses, and refused to take the excuse that Jesus put forth. "The children have to be fed first. It isn't right to take the children's bread and toss it to the dogs" (v. 27) deterred her not at all! She would accept no excuses, no blame, and would take no offense. Instead, she chose a deeper faith. She chose humility. She chose to encounter Jesus on his terms, not on her own.

She would settle for crumbs, and so Jesus gave her the full meal. Unlike the man by the pool, she received so much more than just healing. She engaged with God in playful banter! She received his praise for her faith and her choice to encounter Christ in this unique way. Yes, her daughter was immediately healed, but more than that, she earned Jesus's delight.

The man by the pool would never settle for crumbs. So that's all he received. A few crumbs of healing. He didn't get the blessing, he didn't receive the inner healing. He didn't receive Jesus's delight. Jesus called him to a deeper faith, too, but he refused.

When called by Jesus to the table, the Syrophoenician woman took a step toward him, not away. She went deeper. She encountered. She engaged.

And got more than she knew she wanted.

God's Delight

The healing of her daughter is almost secondary. "Go on home," Jesus says, "The demon has already left your daughter" (Mark 7:29). But before that, Jesus delights in her answer. "Good answer!" the CEB and NLT say, capturing the pleasure of Jesus. Other translations say, "For this saying go thy way" (KJV), "For this statement you may go" (ESV), "For such a reply, you may go" (NIV). The Greek says, "Because of this word, go!" Matthew 15:28 makes it clear that Jesus is praising the woman's faith. It says, "Woman, you have great faith."

When we experience resistance from God, it's not because he doesn't care. When he's silent, it's not because he is scorning us. When he seems harsh, it's not because we're lesser. It's because he's calling us deeper, he's giving us a chance, an opportunity, to come to the table on his terms and find the meal he has prepared for us.

The sense in both the Mark and Matthew versions is that Jesus is not scorning, scolding, or belittling. Instead he's challenging her to rise above preconceived prejudices to engage with him on a new level. And when she does, he delights in her. It almost feels like he throws his head back and laughs with the joy of it.

She will not be deterred. She doesn't need it to happen the way she wants. She doesn't need Jesus to be a certain way or to encounter her in the way she determines. She asks for nothing but to come to the table, whether as a child or a puppy, it doesn't matter, as long as she is near.

So what delights Jesus? Her faith, certainly, but what does that mean? I think he delights in who she is. I think he loves the repartee. I believe he rejoices, *yes, rejoices in her*, because she brings her whole self to him—her wit, her love, her perseverance, her sense of humor. She is humble. She is bold. She wants the healing so desperately that she doesn't try to pretend, she just encounters Jesus with everything she is.

And in doing so, she embodies what it means to "love the Lord your God with all your heart, with all your being, with all your mind, and with all your strength" (Mark 12:30). She brings every part of herself to the feet of Jesus. She encounters him with everything she is.

And to Jesus, to our God, who brings not only healing but a keen delight.

Who Is This God?

Who is this God who invites us to the table with not a compliment but a challenge? Who is he who shakes our worldview with images of dogs and scraps and language that could offend? Who is he who, in our need, waits to see if we will rise to the challenge or simply walk away?

He is the God who Delights.

He is the God of whom it is said:

> Since I know, my God, that you examine the
> mind and take delight in honesty . . .
>
> —1 Chronicles 29:17

The Lord . . . delights in an accurate weight.

—Proverbs 11:1

The vineyard of the Lord of heavenly forces is
the house of Israel,
    and the people of Judah are the plantings in
    which God delighted.

—Isaiah 5:7

But here is my servant, the one I uphold;
    my chosen, who brings me delight.
I've put my spirit upon him;
    he will bring justice to the nations.

—Isaiah 42:1

You will no longer be called Abandoned,
    and your land will no longer be called Deserted.
Instead, you will be called My Delight Is in Her. . . .
    Because the Lord delights in you.

—Isaiah 62:4

No, those who boast should boast in this:
    that they understand and know me.
I am the Lord who acts with kindness,
    justice, and righteousness in the world,
        and I delight in these things, declares the
        Lord.

—Jeremiah 9:24

Who is a God like you, pardoning iniquity,
    overlooking the sin of the few remaining
    for his inheritance?
He doesn't hold on to his anger forever;

he delights in faithful love.

—Micah 7:18

"Don't be afraid, little flock, because your Father
delights in giving you the kingdom."

—Luke 12:32

When we experience resistance from God, it's not because he doesn't care. When he's silent, it's not because he is scorning us. When he seems harsh, it's not because we're lesser. It's because he's calling us deeper, he's giving us a chance, an opportunity, to come to the table on his terms and find the meal he has prepared for us.

He is asking us to engage with him with all our being so that he might encounter all of us, every bit. He is hoping that we will choose to delight.

So what will you do when Jesus doesn't answer in the way you hoped? What will you do when it seems he's ignoring you, putting you off, insulting you? What will you do when your encounter with him is not at all what you expected? Will you step forward and engage with him with everything you are, your whole heart, soul, mind, strength?

Will you take the invitation to go deeper, to delight this God who calls you to more?

If you do, you will find that he is offering so much more than the scraps tossed under the table. He is offering his very self.

Lord, may I come to you with everything I am,
with all you've created me to be.
May I engage with you with all my heart, all my soul, all my mind, all
my strength. Delight in me, Lord, as you invite me to your table.

Jesus took him away from the crowd by himself and put his fingers in the man's ears. Then he spit and touched the man's tongue. Looking into heaven, Jesus sighed deeply and said, "Ephphatha," which means, "Open up." At once, his ears opened, his twisted tongue was released, and he began to speak clearly.

Mark 7:33-35

SEE ALSO MARK 7:31-37.

10

REACHING THROUGH ISOLATION

Ephphatha!

Deafened ears, of sound unconscious,
every passage blocked and closed,
At the word of Christ responding,
all the portals open wide,
Hear with joy friendly voices and
the softly whispered speech.
Every sickness now surrenders,
every listlessness departs,
Tongues long bound by chains of silence
are unloosed and speak aright.

—Prudentius, Hymn 9[1]

Prudentius, Christian poet from the fourth century, captured the wonder of this little story of a man deaf and mostly mute. Deafened ears, bound tongue . . . set free, set right. As I ponder those words I wonder what they mean for me. I can physically hear. I can physically speak. Yet sometimes, especially when life crashes in on me, I don't hear at all. And my speech fails to communicate my heart. Sometimes, I am truly deaf. Sometimes, the things I say aren't right at all.

That's when this little story calls out to me, beckoning me to look a little closer, think a little deeper, and hear the words of my God whispering, "Ephphatha!" Open up! Be opened!

It is possible, even common, to be isolated in the crowd, especially when life is at its hardest.

There are times when that is just what I need to hear from the only One who can save me. I need my ears opened. I need my twisted tongue released. I need my isolation to be broken, away from the crowds in an intimate encounter with God.

I need to open up.

For the man both deaf and mute, it may have happened like this:

A Deaf Man Tells His Story

I am in the midst of a crowd, yet I'm alone. Relatives, friends, people I've known my whole life. They press around me, but I cannot hear them. I cannot speak to them. If I try, my words come out twisted, garbled, and they can't understand what I mean to say.

It is a peculiar isolation.

The crowd is moving, and I with it. My uncle has his hand on my arm. He pulls me forward. My feet scrape the dirt, dust clouds around us. Homes in our city loom ahead.

I know there is noise and talking, the rumble of feet, a cough, a laugh, a few voices louder, sharper than the rest. But I hear none of it. All I hear is the deathly silence.

We travel toward the Sea of Galilee. We stop before we get there, pausing at the edge of town. Wind ruffles my hair. The crowd parts and my uncle tugs me toward a man, a Jew, I think. Perhaps a wandering rabbi.

My uncle is speaking to the man, gesturing. I look away. I don't know what they're saying. Words never reach me in this silence.

But then the man is before me. I startle, and glance up. His eyes search mine, and I am seen. I wonder, then, can he also hear the longing inside me? Can he hear the things I cannot say? The words I hide deep inside.

Gently his hand touches my elbow and he leads me away from the crowd. I glance back at my uncle, and he is smiling. We turn a corner, around a squat building, and the crowd is gone.

It's only this rabbi and I now. The two of us, standing still in the silence.

The man raises his hands. He reaches toward me. I feel his fingers in my ears. They are warm and solid. I can almost hear them.

He withdraws his hands, reaches a finger to his lips, his mouth. He spits and stretches his hand toward me. And I understand. Without a single word, without a single spoken instruction, I know what he is saying to me.

I open my mouth.

He touches my tongue.

He looks toward heaven and I can almost hear his sigh. His lips form a single word, and though I cannot yet hear it, it vibrates through my body, my heart, my soul.

Ephphatha!

My ears are opened. I hear the lingering sound of his voice. I hear the wind across the distant water, I hear the waves on the shores. I hear the voices of those I love, those who love me. I hear them as they become part of my world again. I hear everything.

I open my mouth. I speak. "Thank you." The words are clear, untainted, untwisted. They reflect the gratitude in my soul. "Thank you."

I laugh as I head back to my community, my people, my family, my friends.

"Open up!" he said.

And I see now it was more than a word of healing. It was more than a command to deaf ears and mute tongue. Ephphatha—his command to every part of who I am, who I will now be.

Open up!

Reaching for Wonder

In Jesus's day, there were no hearing aids, no sign language, no schools for the deaf and mute. Instead, those who were deaf were cut off from their community even though they lived within it. They existed in a perpetual silence while the world went on making noise around them. If there was a story to tell, the deaf couldn't hear it. If there was a warning, they didn't know. If someone had a word of encouragement, it remained unheard. And if the mute had something they wanted to communicate, it stayed hidden in their hearts.

Silence was their world. Connection was an abandoned dream.

The deaf man in Mark 7 had plenty of people in his life. Mark 7:32 tells us, "Some people brought to [Jesus] a man who was deaf and could hardly speak, and they begged him to place his hand on the man for healing." The man didn't bring himself to Jesus. He didn't ask Jesus to heal him. Others had to do that, and they were willing to do so.

Often in our own isolation, we have people around us who care about us. They want to bring us to Jesus. They ask him to heal us. They pray, they care, they are longing for us to be able to connect with them in a real way.

Meanwhile we are stuck in silence.

Though we can hear and speak, we are just like the deaf and mute man. He couldn't connect with those around him. Despite the people who wanted to help, to hear, to listen, they couldn't. Even if he wanted to reach out, to hear, to listen, to speak, they couldn't understand him. His isolation was not physical. Mark 7:33 even tells us he was in the midst of a crowd. His, therefore, was an isolation of soul.

So, often, is ours. It is possible, even common, to be isolated in the crowd, especially when life is at its hardest.

Isolated in the Crowd

The deaf man was surrounded by people, but he couldn't hear them. He couldn't hear what they really meant, what they were really trying to communicate to him. When they asked Jesus to "place his hand on the man for healing" (v. 32) he wouldn't know what they were saying. He wouldn't know they were asking for help, for him.

Even though he was surrounded by people who cared for him, he couldn't communicate what was happening in the depths of his soul. He was unable to clearly tell them about his needs, his hopes, his loves, his fears, his worries, his desperation. He could make sounds. His voice was not completely silent, but the text tells us his tongue was "twisted" (v. 35), and even when he tried to speak he couldn't hear how he sounded, he couldn't tell that the words weren't right.

I can relate to that.

I remember it like it was yesterday . . . perhaps because it *was* yesterday. The weight of sick animals, sick kids, type 1 diabetes, college applications for my eldest, wonderful but exhausting events at the ranch, and no time alone for this introvert had finally stopped up my ears and distorted my tongue. I was burdened, irritable, and ready to snap.

Jesus gives us part of himself. He breaks down the barriers between us and God, and between us and others.

My husband came into the room.
I glowered at him.

He said something about the state of the house, something about the floors.

I had just mopped the section he was pointing at.

A few angry, garbled, twisted words later, he was looking at me as if I'd lost my mind. And perhaps I had.

In those moments, I was just as deaf as the man in Mark 7. My speech was probably even more misshapen. I couldn't hear that my husband was actually talking about buying a better vacuum cleaner. I couldn't say that I was just tired and discouraged and needed a rest. I couldn't hear the truth. I couldn't speak it. Instead I said . . . well, I don't even know what I said.

In our own seclusion, when we cannot hear or speak aright, Jesus is not just wanting to heal us, but calling us to be opened, to open up.

What I needed was an encounter with Christ away from the crowd of my worries, my responsibilities, my frustrations and fears.

I needed to have his fingers in my ears and his spit on my tongue. I needed to be touched by the only One who could heal me.

Away from the Crowd

When Jesus healed the deaf man, he did a strange thing. He took him away from the crowd. He removed him from the very people who had brought him to Jesus. Why?

I think it's because we must hear Jesus clearly first before we can hear others. We must have an encounter. The voices of the crowd would have been confusing, difficult, but Jesus took the man away for a moment so the man could focus simply on Jesus. So that in a new kind of quiet, Jesus could touch him.

I love that Jesus used touch to heal the deaf man. I love that he communicated in a way the man could receive. Jesus didn't simply speak a word, which the man couldn't hear. Instead, he poked his fingers in the man's ears. We know that Jesus didn't need to do that to heal. After all, Jesus had just remotely healed the demon-possessed daughter of a Syrophoenician woman a few verses prior.

But this act, the act of putting fingers in a man's ears, was something the man could feel. He could experience it. And he could understand, even though he was deaf. Jesus didn't wait for the man's healing to literally reach out and connect with him. Jesus broke through this man's isolation through touch.

Next, Jesus spat and touched the man's tongue. It sounds rather disgusting, and yet more is happening here than it may at first seem. In spitting and touching, Jesus shared a part of himself to make a solid connection with the man who was isolated in the crowd. Jesus's own spit mixed with the man's on the mute man's tongue. The symbolism is deep.

Just as Jesus died on the cross and rose again, defeating death to give us life in him, just as he puts his life in us when we are born again, in this story of a deaf man healed, Jesus also gives part of himself to bridge the gap between sickness and healing, to put his life into another in order to make him whole. He wouldn't have had to do it that way, but he did. I believe he chose this method of healing because putting part of his life into us is how our isolation ends, not just physically but spiritually. Jesus gives us part of himself. He breaks down the barriers between us and God, and between us and others.

Be Opened!

Then he speaks a single word: *Ephphatha!* Open, open up, be opened! It is a command.

Mark uses the Aramaic word *Ephphatha* so we, thousands of years later, can hear it just as Jesus spoke it. Typically, the Gospel writers don't bother with the Aramaic when relating the words Jesus spoke. But Mark does it here because it's important that we hear and we speak. Clearly.

We have to step out of the crowd and encounter the living God. We need to stop hiding the truth about ourselves, our situation, our fears, hopes, failures, dreams.

Just as he did for the deaf man, Jesus takes us away from the crowd so that we, too, can hear, really hear, the word that Jesus speaks not only to the man, but to us. No muddling, no confusion, no translation.

A single word that echoes down through the millennia and into our hearts: *Ephphatha!*

Mark gives us a clear picture of the passion behind that single word. Before he spoke it, Jesus looked up to heaven. Then, he sighed. The word used for "sigh" is the same one we read in Romans 8:26, which says, "In the same way, the Spirit comes to help our weakness. We don't know what we should pray, but the Spirit himself pleads our case with unexpressed groans." Unexpressed groans. The ESV translates it "groanings too deep for words." Everything that Jesus did for this man has led to this moment, to this single command: *Ephphatha!*

Jesus's sigh, his unutterable groan, is not about simple healing. He could have done that from a distance, with a simple word, with a glance. But this command, this order to "Open up!" goes far deeper. For the man, and for us.

For the deaf man, this was not just an opening of the ears and loosening of the tongue physically, but a call to be open to really hear, to truly speak, clearly. It was a call to come out of isolation.

In our own seclusion, when we cannot hear or speak aright, Jesus is not just wanting to heal us, but calling us to be opened, to open up. When life is at its worst, when we're isolated in the crowd, when we can't hear what others are trying to say, when our own words are twisted with sin or grief or bitterness or sorrow, Jesus draws us into an intimate encounter with him. He puts fingers in our ears, spits and touches our tongue. And he has one command: Be opened.

With that single word, he is calling us out of hiddenness, to hear the truth, to speak the truth. Clearly. Honestly. Fully. Without a single twist or spin. Michael Card says, "Jesus's groaning words, 'Be opened,' represent the deepest hope of the gospel: that you and I might truly hear and eventually clearly speak the good news."[2] But there's more to it than that.

Jesus commands us, just as he did the deaf man, to "open up" not just to the gospel but in every aspect of our lives. We are to live with hearing ears and a tongue that speaks clearly the truth. We are not to live in isolation in a crowd any longer. John 8:32 says, "Then you will know the truth, and the truth will set you free."

Jesus is sighing, groaning, longing for us to open up so that we may be more than healed. We may be free.

Who Is This God?

Who is this God who does more than heal? Who is he who is not satisfied to repair the deaf and make the mute speak? Who is he who calls us to deeper listening, deeper speaking? Who is he who opens more than physical ears, untwists more than physical tongues?

He is the God of Ephphatha. He is the God of *aletheia*.

Aletheia is the Greek word for truth. It also means unhidden. Exposed. No longer in isolation.

When we can't hear God or others clearly, when our words don't rightly reflect the longing and need in our souls, the answer is not to pretend, to blend in with the crowd, to hide in plain sight. The answer is ephphatha. It is aletheia.

We have to step out of the crowd and encounter the living God. We need to stop hiding the truth about ourselves, our situation, our fears, hopes, failures, dreams.

We need to declare with Isaiah: "Mourn for me; I'm ruined! I'm a man with unclean lips, and I live among a people with unclean lips. Yet I've seen the king, the Lord of heavenly forces!" (Isaiah 6:5).

We need to confess with David after his sin with Bathsheba, and his betrayal of Uriah the Hittite: "I know my wrongdoings, my sin is always right in front of me. I've sinned against you. . . . I've committed evil in your sight. . . . And yes, you want truth in the most hidden places; you teach me wisdom in the most secret space. . . . Create a clean heart for me, God; put a new, faithful spirit deep inside me!" (Psalm 51:3-6, 10).

We need to sing with ex-slave-trader John Newton who wrote:

> *Amazing grace! How sweet the sound*
> *That saved a wretch like me!*
> *I once was lost, but now am found;*
> *Was blind, but now I see.*

I was deaf but now I hear. I was mute but now I speak. Hear the truth. Speak the truth. Don't hide any longer.

As I write these words, my own soul sighs within me because there are people dear to me who need ephphatha, who need aletheia. I groan for those who want to hide and pretend everything's OK, they're OK, when everything is far from fine. I sigh for those who want to deny they even need real healing, that they need Jesus's fingers in their ears, his spit on their tongues. They persist in deafness and muteness when their life is imploding. No matter how loud we shout, no matter how we crowd around them, they cannot hear, they will not speak. And their souls are withering beneath the weight of isolation and sin.

And Jesus is calling out—Ephphatha! Open up! Just open up! There is healing, there is freedom, to be found in that simple, spoken command.

Ephphatha . . .

Lord . . .

"Strengthen the weak hands,
    and support the unsteady knees.
Say to those who are panicking:
    'Be strong! Don't fear!
Here's your God . . .
    God will come to save you.'
Then the eyes of the blind will be opened,
    and the ears of the deaf will be cleared.
Then the lame will leap like the deer,
    and the tongue of the speechless will sing.
Waters will spring up in the desert,
    and streams in the wilderness."
                    —Isaiah 35:3-6

This is my prayer.

"If you can do anything, help us! Show us compassion!"
Jesus said to him, "'If you can do anything'? All things
are possible for the one who has faith." At that the boy's
father cried out, "I have faith; help my lack of faith!"

Mark 9:22-24

SEE ALSO MARK 9:14-29.

11

Reaching Through Failure

A Demon-Possessed Son

You've tried everything. You've brought it to God. You've prayed. You've asked others to pray. You've hoped. You've acted. You've reached for God. You've even brought your need to the elders in the church and tried to do just what the Bible instructs. You've done it all. And still . . .

Failure.

Nothing works. Nothing changes. Despite all you've tried. Despite all the prayers and hopes and assurances that all will be well.

It's not well.

What does it look like to encounter God when everything we thought should work hasn't, when we're out of options, when we believe but are drowning in unbelief? When we have faith but it's failing us?

Sometimes I think it would be easier if we were doing something wrong. That way we could point to the problem and say, "That's the reason for failure. Fix it, and God will heal, God will work, this pain and fear and discouragement and desperation will be over." But often, that's not the case. Sometimes we've done everything just as well as we know how. And still everything we try fails.

Nothing. Changes.

Now what? What do we do in the face of failure and fear? What does Jesus do?

What does it look like to encounter God when everything we thought should work hasn't, when we're out of options, when we believe but are drowning in unbelief? When we have faith but it's failing us?

For the man whose son was possessed by a destructive spirit, it may have happened like this:

─ A Father Tells His Story ─

They surround me like birds from the sea. Squawking, flapping, pecking at the remains of my faith. Experts in the law, neighbors in the crowd, followers of the rabbi called Jesus, the one from Nazareth. They all shout, argue, flail about with words and arms in an assault that drives into my very soul.

Jesus is not among them. He isn't even here.

But my son is. My poor, beleaguered son. He stands beside me, hunched and staring at the ground with glazed eyes. He is calm now, for this moment. But the demon could overpower him at any moment. It could kill him. It's tried so many times.

This life we live . . . this life of hoping and waiting, of last-minute rescues and panting terror and desperate fights against the evil that consumes him. It is a life of watching and trembling and trying to find a way to free him.

A life of failing and fear.

Today is no different.

Failure.

I had such hope. They said the Healer could make him well. They said he had sent out seventy of his followers and they had healed the sick, cast out demons, released captives such as my son. I saw them too. I heard the townspeople whisper that the prophecies in Isaiah were coming true. And I dared to hope. I dared to believe.

I dared to bring my son to the foot of this mountain and ask that he be healed.

Too bad the teachers of the law came with me. Too bad the crowds followed.

Too bad that those who went into the towns and country-side to bring hope, to heal, to set free, could not do so today.

Too bad that when I brought them my son, they could not free him.

Too bad they failed.

I failed.

I don't know what else can be done. But they don't care what I think. They don't listen to what I say. Instead, they argue, they bicker, they peck over the rotten bits of failure and the carcass of law they claim to uphold. And meanwhile my son stands here, in horrific silence, unable to say a single word, silenced by the evil spirit within him, the spirit that wants nothing more than to destroy him.

And I wonder, if Jesus's disciples were less focused on proving their master's worth, would they have been able to cast the demon from my son? If they looked to their master's God instead of looking to defend him, would my boy now be free?

I place my arm around my child's shoulders and draw him closer. He stiffens beneath my touch. The crowd shifts, mumbles. I drop my arm and move forward.

"He comes. Look!" A man from the crowd points toward the mountain.

The crowd starts to run. I run with them. They murmur, talk, chatter with excitement. I don't say a word.

Then I see him, the healing rabbi. He descends the hill with three of his closest followers. He almost seems to glow. But no, that can't be. It is just the remnants of sunlight glinting off his robe. Or perhaps it's the remnants of my hope that glitter and fade but refuse to die.

Maybe . . . no. Everything I've tried, everything I've hoped, has ended in failure. How can I hope again?

Jesus stops. The crowd stops. The murmurs die down. Jesus lifts a hand and my neighbors fall silent. He raises his voice just a bit to be heard. "What are you arguing about?"

The teachers of the law don't answer. His disciples don't answer either.

I elbow my way forward. "Teacher," I call.

He turns his gaze toward me. I stop when I see the anger in his eyes. But it's not anger directed at me. It is an inner burning. And for a moment I wonder if it is not anger at all. Perhaps it is hope.

I draw in my breath and try to put into words the agony of my soul. "Teacher, I brought my son to you, since he has a spirit that doesn't allow him to speak." Emotions surge within me. I crush them down. "Wherever it overpowers him, it throws him into a fit. He foams at the mouth, grinds his teeth, and stiffens up."

Jesus waits, watches me. I know what he is asking. I know he wants me to speak not of my son's condition but of the failure that poisons my soul. I swallow and meet his gaze. "So I . . . I spoke to your disciples to see if they could throw it out, but . . ." There is always a *but*. "But they couldn't." Does he hear the pain behind my simple words? Does he hear the frustration, hopelessness? Does he hear the death of my faith?

I dared to believe. And here I stand with the son I love, and the destructive spirit that remains in him. Here I stand in failure. Again.

Jesus doesn't answer me. He answers them. His gaze leaves me and pierces those who bicker and argue. His words are sharp, like swords, as he says, "You faithless generation, how long will I be with you? How long will I put up with you? Bring him to me."

Bring him?

The crowd parts, and others bring him forward. My son lifts his head, but something else glints from his eyes as he peers at Jesus. I know that something. I know it too well.

Oh no.

My son, my beloved boy, falls to the ground. He rolls around. His mouth foams as the fit overtakes him. I start toward him but Jesus lays a hand on my arm.

"How long has this been going on?"

Why is Jesus so calm? Where is the fear, the panic, the desperation that rages in me? Why is it not reflected in him? Why is his calm not reflected in me? Perhaps I have become used to the panic. Perhaps this is a too-familiar fear.

This time when I answer, my voice shakes, my hands clench, my eyes dart from Jesus to my boy. "Since he was a child!" I nearly shriek the words. Why isn't anyone doing anything? Why isn't anyone helping? Why isn't Jesus? Doesn't he care? "It has often thrown him into a fire or into water trying to kill him!" He isn't faking. This is real! And if we don't stop it MY SON COULD DIE RIGHT HERE, RIGHT NOW. Can he hear my silent screams? I almost reach out and grab his robe. "If you can do anything, help us! Show us compassion!" *Please, please. . . .* I fall silent. I have no more words. I don't even know why I asked him. I don't know if he can do anything. I don't know if there will ever be any hope for this life we live, for the life of my son.

I just don't know anymore.

Then Jesus speaks, his tone quiet, firm, gentle. Not condemning but questioning, perhaps calling. Will I hear his call? "'If you can do anything'?" He repeats my words, and I know he is handing them back to me, giving me the choice to claim them or cast them away. He smiles then, so subtly that I almost miss it. "All things are possible for the one who has faith."

I catch my breath. Time seems to slow. He has seen the war in my soul. How could he have known? How could he have known that all the failures, all the disappointments, have created this war within me that I don't know how to win? All I can do is name it. All I can do is give voice to the battle within.

And so I do. "I have faith; help my lack of faith!"

For a moment, Jesus meets my gaze. He doesn't condemn my faithlessness. He doesn't applaud my stumbling faith. He simply gives me an almost imperceptible nod. And I know that by speaking the truth in all its confused ugliness, I have somehow answered his call.

The crowd begins to surge forward, toward us. Jesus turns away from me, toward my frothing, rolling son. Then, Jesus's voice turns harsh. He speaks not to my son, but to the unclean spirit within him. "Mute and deaf spirit, I command you to come out of him and never enter him again."

A scream tears from my child's throat, rips through my father-heart. Convulsions shake him until I think they will break him. And then he is still.

The spirit is gone, but he is so very still and quiet and pale.

"Is he dead?" Whispers snake through the crowd. "I think he's dead." "He must have died."

But Jesus leans over and takes my boy's hand. He lifts him up, and my boy stands. Alive. Well. He touches a hand to his ear and grins. Then he looks at me and says a single word. "Father."

And I know that it was not my faith that overcame failure. It was the faithfulness of him who called me from my fear.

My son runs into my arms, and I squeeze him tight. I whisper to him the first words he will be able to hear. I whisper them and fill them with all my wonder.

"Jesus has set us free."

Reaching for Wonder

Failure. As I sit down to write today, a text dings on my computer. An ex-business partner of someone close to me has died. The two parted on poor terms and never reconciled. Now it's too late. Failure. I glance over at my email inbox to a message telling me that another friend's husband is still insisting on divorce, despite going to counseling. Failure. I know I shouldn't but I click on a social-media newsfeed and see condolences for another friend along with the name of her son. She lost her husband in an accident just a couple of years ago. Heartbreak.

How often have I felt that I couldn't find Jesus when I needed him most? I come to him in desperation, I cry out, and am met with silence.

I think about all the pain in the world, just in my small little world of friends, even just in my own life and family. I think about how we try and pray and strive and hope to make things better, and how often we fail. How often the pain worsens, how hard it is to keep trying, how heavy the weight of discouragement can become.

Enough to crush us.

And then I think of a father with his demon-inflicted son. I think of the anguish of trying to keep that boy alive, of dragging him out of the fire, snuffing out the flames on his clothes, treating the burns so they don't become infected, and trying not to weep at the futility of it all. I think of the desperation of hauling him out of the water when limbs are flailing and liquid has sucked into his lungs, of listening to the gurgling gasps for air, the frantic thrashing. I think about the constant watching, praying, hoping against hope that it won't happen again, that it won't happen today. That maybe today he will be safe.

But he's not.

Like any father, I'm sure he would rather have the demon inflict him instead of his son. He would rather endure the pain himself, if only his child could be free. But that's not an option. His son is not free. And so he isn't either.

Imagine the fear this father lives in every single day. Is today the day the evil spirit will win? Is today the day it will succeed in burning him in the fire, drowning him in the lake, destroying him? Imagine the constant vigilance, to never rest, never take a break, never let down his guard or the monster might strike and devour his son.

At any moment, any moment at all, the foaming, the writhing, the danger and horror could come again, and again, and again. The father would have tried everything to have his son freed from this spirit. He would have tried doctors, healers, pray-ers and priests. Nothing helped. And then he brought his boy to Jesus, a last chance, a final hope.

And Jesus wasn't there.

How often have I felt that I couldn't find Jesus when I needed him most? I come to him in desperation, I cry out, and am met with silence.

I take my pain to his followers, but they can't help. Sometimes they are too busy arguing with the Pharisees.

For this father, these were the same disciples who had cast out demons before. In Luke 10, we read about how Jesus sent out seventy-two of his followers to spread the good news. Luke 10:17

tells us, "The seventy-two returned joyously, saying, 'Lord, even the demons submit themselves to us in your name.'"

But this time, the demon is not submitting. This time it won't come out.

Failure upon failure upon failure. And failure again.

And then Jesus comes down from the mountain.

The crowd rushes toward him, and within it, a father, a son, a deaf-and-mute demon, and a challenge to try again.

Can the father muster his faith one more time? Can he encounter this rabbi, this healer, this Jesus when his followers failed? Does he dare?

He does. With his limping faith, with his son no better than he's ever been, he does. He speaks out of the crowd, he separates himself from it and comes forward.

He doesn't hide but talks frankly of the latest failure. Mark 9:17-18 records his words to Jesus: "Teacher, I brought my son to you. . . . I spoke to your disciples to see if they could throw it out, but they couldn't."

There is the tension we all experience —
this war within between faith and fear,
hope and despair, belief and failure.

I can feel the pain behind those words, the disappointment, the hopelessness, the fear. Maybe it would never be cast out. Maybe there was no one, nothing, that could help. Maybe this kind of demon would haunt them, hunt them, until his son was destroyed.

Maybe his case was special and there was no hope for freedom.

What's Jesus Mad About?

I expect Jesus to answer with compassion. I expect a gentle reply to this hurting dad. But that's not what happens. Jesus offers a rebuke. A harsh rebuke. He says, "You faithless generation, how long will I be with you? How long will I put up with you?" (v. 19).

The answer startles me, disturbs me. How can this be?

But then I notice a little word, *autois* is the Greek "them." The text doesn't say that Jesus answered the father. Instead, it specifically says, "Jesus answered *them*" (emphasis mine). Jesus turns his attention from the man to the crowd, to those surrounding him, and to his disciples and the teachers of the law who, in the face of this man's desperation, have been bickering with one another. Jesus also includes the lookie-loos, those who came just to see what would happen. These he calls faithless. These are the ones about whom he says, "How long will I put up with you?"

They argue and defend, but they don't weep . . . what kind of faith is that!?

The father comes out of the crowd. He speaks to Jesus. He dares to try again in the face of failure. But the disciples, who were moments before arguing so vehemently with the teachers of the law, are suddenly silent. How is it that they aren't running to Jesus to ask for help in healing the man's son? How is it that the friends and neighbors who run to Jesus in excitement are not pushing the son forward and begging for healing?

Why is only the father speaking? Why is he who has faced failure upon failure the only one to try again?

What's Jesus mad about? I think he's mad because his followers cared more about defending their faith than exhibiting it. They cared more about arguing than about a father and son in need. And because of that, they failed.

Failure and Faith—The War Within

They failed a man who needed them. But what about that man's faith? What about the faith of the father?

The crowd brings the boy forward when Jesus asks for him. As soon as they do, the evil spirit sees Jesus and immediately takes over. It throws the boy down; he rolls around stiff and foaming at the mouth.

I believe that's because Jesus not only freed the son from the demon but freed the father from the war between fear and faith.

What the father fears most happens right in front of him . . . again. All the failure, all the pain, all the horror hits as the son he loves falls and foams.

And Jesus does nothing to stop it. He does nothing to prevent the man's fear or hide the failure. Instead, he turns back to the father and asks a simple question, "How long has this been going on?" (v. 21).

I am struck by the lack of panic, lack of hurry, in Jesus. While he interacts with the father, the boy continues to flop and seize. The tension of that moment must have been overwhelming, especially for the father. But Jesus is in no rush.

The father is able to answer. "Since he was a child. It has often thrown him into a fire or into water trying to kill him." Reviewing the fear seems to heighten it, for the man then bursts out, "If you can do anything, help us! Show us compassion!" (v. 22). I imagine he is shouting these words.

But Jesus doesn't shout back. Instead, he calls the man deeper. At the height of the man's fear and failure, Jesus asks him to focus not on his son, who is having a life-threatening fit at their feet, but on Jesus and faith. "'If you can do anything?'" Jesus asks. "All things are possible for the one who has faith" (v. 23).

This isn't the first time we see Jesus calling a hurting person to a deeper faith when he or she is at the pinnacle of pain. It seems like an impossible request, and yet it is common for Jesus (remember Jairus) to focus on faith when we are filled with the fear of our failures.

And I love the man's response: "I have faith; help my lack of faith!" or as it translates from the Greek, "I believe! Help my unbelief!" (v. 24).

There is the tension we all experience—this war within between faith and fear, hope and despair, belief and failure.

Jesus honors the battle. Earlier, he expressed his frustration at the lack of faith of his disciples, the teachers of the law, and the crowd. But here there is no such condemnation. There's no scorn, no rebuke, not even any disappointment from Jesus.

Why? This father doesn't have model faith, and he knows it. He knows it. And that seems to be the key. Jesus's words were never meant to shame him, to say, "Well, I could heal if your faith was just *good enough*." Instead they were meant to gently invite him to confront his own inner war, his own tension between his faith and fear, and do it at the moment when his fear was strongest, when his son was in the throes of a demon-possessed fit. Jesus was giving him the opportunity to bring the inner war to Jesus and be freed.

Because that's exactly what Jesus does next. He doesn't respond to the man at all. He simply casts out the demon, so violently that the boy appears to be dead. It's a scary healing, a frightening freedom, but a full freedom. For both of them.

The son is freed from the demon. And the father is freed from his failure and fear. We know that because there is a final test for the father. The boy is still, and several in the crowd start whispering that the boy has died. His son's death was what the father most feared. It would be the final failure. And here his son lies. Still as death. Pale as death.

Sometimes, you just have to keep walking. You just have to dare to hope again, believe again. You have to hold to the wisps of faith you have and be honest about the faith you lack.

And we don't hear a single word from the father.

I believe that's because Jesus not only freed the son from the demon but freed the father from the war between fear and faith.

The foolish crowd believes Jesus's healing resulted in the boy's death. The father knows better. He waits. He watches. He submits to whatever Jesus will do. Why? Because he's not only placed his faith in Jesus's hands, but he has also placed his lack of faith there. His belief *and* his unbelief. He brings it all and gives it to Jesus with the simply cry, "I have faith; help my lack of faith!" And that is enough.

It's enough for us too.

Winning the War Within

Every year we do a Haunted Trail event the weekend before Halloween at the charity ranch I run. We do it because in our lives, and in the lives of our guests (disadvantaged kids from all over the city), there are many things to fear. There's a lot of failure. The trail begins with a sign from the book of Job that reads, "The thing that I fear comes upon me" (Job 3:25 ESV). It ends with a sign saying, "Who will rescue me from this . . . death?" (Romans 7:24 NIV). The final sign points to a huge wooden cross.

Unlike some, we don't choose to ignore Halloween. We choose to transform it. Often life is like a haunted trail. The thing we fear comes upon us. Death comes, cobwebs invade, evil scratches at the corners of our lives trying to defeat us. Sometimes we have a child flirting with death and nothing we do helps. Sometimes we have a financial, health, relational, marital, spiritual crisis and all we can see are bones and scary glowing eyes along the path of our lives. Sometimes we fail. Sometimes we fear. And that's the trail we walk. But the trail doesn't end with a graveyard. It doesn't end with a skeletal horse and rider. It ends with the cross. It ends with hope. And sometimes, you just have to keep walking. You just have to dare to hope again, believe again. You have to hold to the wisps of faith you have and be honest about the faith you lack.

So, the question is: Do you dare to try again? Ask again? Hope again? Do you dare to be honest about the war within?

God does not scorn us in our failure and our desperation. He invites us deeper. He invites us to bring to him not only our faith but our failures, in all their ignominy. Lay it all out before him, and then be quiet, watch, wait.

Perhaps the son is not dead. Perhaps you both can be free.

Who Is This God?

God isn't just the God of our faith. He is the God of our lack of faith. He is the God of the War Within.

In 1 Kings 18, Elijah led an amazing victory over the prophets of Baal. He called and God answered. His offering was consumed, the water licked up around it, and God was proven to be the one true God. Four hundred and fifty prophets of Baal died. Elijah won. And then, in 1 Kings 19, Elijah ran from the wicked Queen Jezebel and hid in a cave. Then, he despaired. Then, he feared. He failed. God was God in his victory. God was God in his failure. He never stopped using Elijah to proclaim his truth. God was the God of Elijah's war within.

All the confusion, the regret, the pain, the tension and conflicting thoughts and feelings that sometimes rage within us— he wants to be the God of it all.

In Matthew 16, Mark 8, and Luke 9, Jesus asks his disciples, "Who do you say that I am?" In a glorious moment of faith, Peter declares, "You are the Messiah!" A few verses later when Jesus is talking about his death and resurrection, Peter starts to scold and correct Jesus. Jesus says to him, "Get behind me, Satan! You are not thinking God's thoughts but human thoughts" (Mark 8:33). Ouch! Peter feared. He failed. God was God in his victory, and God was still God when he failed. And Peter still became the rock that Jesus promised he'd be. God was the God of Peter's war within.

And then there's Mary, Jesus's mother, who faithfully and boldly proclaimed to the angel who told her she was to bear the Messiah though she was a virgin, "I am the Lord's servant. Let it be with me just as you have said" in Luke 1:38. Then, in Mark 3 she and Jesus's brothers come to take control of him because they say, "He's out of his mind!" (Mark 3:21). Later we find her weeping at the foot of the cross. Mary, who was called the most blessed among women, feared, failed, and had faith. And God always remained the God of her war within.

God is not surprised, offended, disappointed or put off when we fail. He does not shame us when we cry out, "I have faith! Help my lack of faith!" He simply asks that we bring it all to him. All the confusion, the regret, the pain, the tension and conflicting thoughts and feelings that sometimes rage within us—he wants to be the God of it all.

So, when all else has failed, when we've failed, Jesus whispers, "All things are possible for the one who has faith," knowing that we don't have the faith it will take to set us free.

But he is enough. In our weakness, failure, and unbelief, he is always still enough.

Lord, I believe. Help my unbelief! Be the God of my war within.
I am not proud of my faith. I see its weaknesses.
But still, may I come to you.
May I cling to you when I've failed.
May I try again, hope again, believe again.
I will watch and wait for you when everything seems lost.

"Whoever hasn't sinned should throw the first stone."
Bending down again, he wrote on the ground. Those
who heard him went away, one by one, beginning with
the elders. Finally, only Jesus and the woman were left in
the middle of the crowd. Jesus stood up and said to her,
"Woman, where are they? Is there no one to condemn
you?" She said, "No one, sir." Jesus said, "Neither
do I condemn you. Go, and from now on, don't sin
anymore."

John 8:7-11

SEE ALSO JOHN 8:1-11.

12

REACHING THROUGH GUILT

The First Stone

Sometimes it's not your fault. But sometimes it is. Sometimes the pain, hurt, and horribleness in your life are caused by your own mistakes, your own choices, your own sin. Sometimes, you're to blame.

What does it look like to encounter Jesus then? What does he do when we come to him with self-inflicted pain? What does he do when everyone around us is ready to throw stones, and stones are what we deserve?

Sin isn't the result of a meanie-god forbidding fun. Sin is sin because it destroys us and others.

Blame, guilt, shame. Do we avoid them? Do we own up to them? Do we deny, suppress, or scorn them? Or do we simply stand before Jesus and wait for what he will do in the face of our fault?

For the woman caught in the act of adultery, it might have happened like this:

A Guilty Woman Tells Her Story

They push me. They drag me. They shove me toward the temple. Not all of them, some won't even touch me. But their presence looms. I cannot escape. I can't run from their condemnation. I can't run from my guilt.

They caught me in his bed. They caught me in my sin. They caught me at dawn.

There is no hope for me now.

I stumble toward a man teaching in the temple courts. He sits and the people funnel toward him. Morning sunlight splashes across the courtyard. I blink in the light.

All the people gather around him. They push me to the center of the group, then they confront the man. He stands.

"Teacher!" a Pharisee demands, "This woman was caught in the act of committing adultery."

I can almost hear the sneer in his voice, but . . . but the sneer is not directed toward me. Who is this man who teaches in the temple courts? Who is he who is hated more than I?

"In the Law," another continues, "Moses commanded us to stone women like this. What do you say?"

So smug. Almost gloating. All those who brought me are gloating. And suddenly, I understand. This isn't about me at all.

They don't care about my sin. I am only a pawn in some game they are playing. A game meant not so much to condemn me, to catch me, as to catch and condemn him.

I expect him to agree with them. I expect to be stoned. I see the stones in their hands. They brought them. They hold them now. The time has come. I'm going to die. Fear rises like bile in my throat. I choke on it.

But this man doesn't say a word. Instead, he bends down and begins to write on the ground with his finger.

They continue to harass him, badger him into answering.

I sway on my feet. How long will it take for me to die? Will the rocks kill me quickly? Or will they just keep piling up until I die a slow, agonizing death? How long before someone throws the first stone?

"Well? Answer us!" they demand. There is glee in their voices. Why should there be glee when we are here because of sin, my sin, my death?

Or perhaps we're here because of theirs.

Finally, the man stands. He spares them hardly a glance and tosses out his answer as if he is speaking about which fish to choose for dinner. "Whoever hasn't sinned should throw the first stone," he says. Simple as that. And then he bends down and starts writing again with his finger in the dirt. Writing as if he hasn't a care in the world.

I wait for who will throw the first rock. I wait for it to hit me, hurt me.

He continues to write. I can't see what he is scribbling there in the dust. Maybe it doesn't matter. He writes.

I tremble, my hair falling over my face.

And then I hear the first stone drop. Footsteps fade away. And another stone drops.

I swallow and glance up. They are leaving. The oldest leave first. Then the middle-aged. Then the younger ones. One by one every person walks away. And then it is only he and I left in the middle of a crowd of onlookers. And even they back away.

He stands and his gaze pierces mine. "Woman." He says the term so gently that I begin to weep. "Where are they? Is there no one to condemn you?"

I draw a shuddering breath and answer, "No one, sir."

He nods. "Neither do I condemn you. Go, and from now on, don't sin anymore."

I choke on my tears; I choke on impossible hope. Moments ago, I was surrounded by stones in the hands of those who would kill me. Moments ago, I had nothing but my sin and my guilt. Moments ago, I stood condemned. And now . . . now . . . the stones have fallen.

And I know that the one who could condemn me has chosen another way.

Who is this one who frees me from the stain of sin?

Who is he who stands in the center of the stones?

Reaching for Wonder

The story of the woman caught in adultery is what scholars call a textual floater. In other words, it's not entirely clear where this story should be placed in the Gospels, or even if it should be included at all. The earliest manuscripts of the Gospels do not include this story. A few later manuscripts include the story in Luke. However, thematically and stylistically, it fits best here in John where it most frequently shows up in later manuscripts. Augustine (AD 354–430) believed it had been removed from earlier manuscripts for fear it would encourage adultery, especially for women. While the placement of the *Pericope Adulterae* is in question, most scholars, both ancient and modern, believe this story to be authentic and circulated by the original apostles. It is consistent with the character of Christ that we see throughout the Gospel accounts and was most likely shared in various settings in the spread of the gospel orally by the apostles.

For our purposes, we will consider this encounter with Christ from the perspective of the woman who was caught in her sin, dragged in front of Jesus, and unable to deny or squirm away from her guilt.

Sin Makes Us Pawns

After all, unlike so many of the hurting people we've highlighted in this book, the woman caught in adultery didn't come to Jesus on her own accord. She was forced to the temple and into the presence of Christ by Jesus's enemies. She wasn't brought there for forgiveness, redemption, help, or hope. She was a pawn in the conflict between the Pharisees and Jesus.

That is the very nature of sin. It keeps us from the temple; it keeps us from Jesus. It keeps us from going to God on our own. And worse, it makes us pawns in the evil schemes of those who oppose Christ.

Sin isn't the result of a meanie-god forbidding fun. Sin is sin because it destroys us and others. If it were good for us, it wouldn't be sin. But God outlines certain acts, such as adultery, as sin because they are poison to us and they make us victims of the enemies of Christ and of our souls. We use sin instead of him to fill the emptiness and need inside us, and in doing so we open ourselves to destruction. The scribes and the Pharisees were eager to sacrifice this woman's life in order to catch Jesus in a condemning conundrum. She didn't matter to them at all. They only wanted to use her to find a way to accuse Jesus.

But what she didn't realize, what they didn't realize, was that in bringing a sinner to Jesus they also brought themselves. She encountered Christ. And so did they.

So there she stood, because of her own sin, to be used by others for their own ungodly purposes, used by people who really didn't care if she lived or died. To them, she was less than human. She was not a person at all.

The only one who saw her was the one she was being used to trap.

In our own lives, sin often feels good. It often seems like the only way to feel whole. But it always results in our dehumanization and victimization. The girl who gives herself in sex before marriage is used by the man who seduces her. The guy who cheats at work to get ahead becomes a slave of his bosses, who can push him to sin more. The woman who gossips gets gossiped about. The man who compares himself to others, always needing to be "better than," becomes the unknowing lapdog of those to whom he's comparing himself and must follow them instead of Jesus. And the list goes on. Pornography, jealousy, fits of rage, racism, pride, arrogance . . . all will make us pawns in someone else's game and ultimately in the game of our enemy.

The only way to get free of the game is to stand in front of Jesus, accept the blame, and wait for the first stone.

Throwing Stones

An interesting thing happens when Jesus answers the experts in the law, with their stones in hand. He says, "Whoever hasn't sinned should throw the first stone" (v. 7), and one by one, starting with the oldest, they drop their stones and walk away. None of the stones are thrown. They were ready, they were in hand. But all were dropped. Every single one of them.

Typically, we think that these scribes and Pharisees realized that they too were sinners and in a moment of rare repentance, they dropped their rocks and left the scene. Possibly. But it does seem rather odd that this group that was so intent on finding a way to condemn Jesus would now just meekly meander off because they saw they were sinners. Something more must be going on here.

The woman stood in their midst, caught in adultery, no excuses, no hiding, no way out. The law in Deuteronomy 22:22-24 states that a man and woman caught in adultery should be killed (not necessarily stoned as the scribes and Pharisees assert). Roman law didn't allow for Jews to carry out capital punishment. Still, the stones were ready, and the accusers were prepared to call Jesus a law-breaker either way.

Freedom is found in embracing the truth even when it's hard to hear and harder to accept. Even when others are standing around us, ready to pelt us with stones.

They had their plan. The adulteress was caught. And with her, they believed Jesus was caught as well.

There is no way she could not have seen the trap laid out for her, and for Jesus. There is no way she could have foreseen that she could get them to drop their stones.

But what she didn't realize, what they didn't realize, was that in bringing a sinner to Jesus they also brought themselves. She encountered Christ. And so did they.

And that's why they dropped their rocks.

In our lives, too, we cannot get others to drop their stones. Only Jesus can do that. Only Jesus.

Sometimes, like the woman, we are to blame, we are at fault, we have been foolish, we have sinned. And now we are encircled by others seeking to throw stones. Our tendency is to shift blame, point to others, get the attention off ourselves in an effort to save ourselves from the stones. We want to protect ourselves by saying, "It's not my fault!" even though it is, or "It's not *all* my fault," which may be true. But blame-shifting won't get others to drop their rocks. Blame-shifting, even though it's often our go-to strategy for self-preservation, will only gather more stones.

Only Jesus can intervene. Only he can save us from a stoning.

But not if we don't face our sin.

I'm reminded of an incident that occurred when my oldest daughter was nine. I remember it well. I glared at the cabinet door that sat mangled on the carpet in front of me and shouted for my three-year-old. "Jayna, get in here!"

Jayna came running.

I stabbed my finger at the broken door. "Did you do that?" It was a good guess that Jayna was the culprit, even though she had four other siblings. Of all the things broken in the house, Jayna had caused 95 percent of them. We didn't call her "little monkey" for nothing. So, when something turned up broken, Jayna was the first one I called.

But this time, she didn't hide her face and pretend she didn't understand. Instead, she looked at me with wide, innocent eyes and said, "Bet-a-nee break it."

I frowned. "Are you sure?"

Jayna smiled. "Yes. Bet-a-nee do it."

I called for Bethany. A moment later she appeared before me. I motioned toward the door. "Do you know how that got broken?"

She didn't answer.

"Did you do it?"

"No."

I frowned.

She fidgeted.

I bent over and picked up the door.

Her face turned red. Then, she started to bawl. "Yes, I did it. I did it," she hollered. Between sobs, she told how she sat on the door just like we'd told her not to do, and it broke, and she lied, and, and, and . . . and she didn't want to get in trouble. *Waaaa . . .*

Once the sobbing subsided, Bethany and I settled in for a good talk. We discussed how Mommy and Daddy are wise. It's best to do what we say. And if you fail to obey and do something stupid, it's best to fess up right away. Otherwise you end up carrying your mistake around with you and allowing others to throw stones.

Sometimes we sit on the doors in our lives and they are broken. Sometimes it's our own fault. But freedom isn't found in hiding or letting others take the blame. Freedom is found in embracing the truth even when it's hard to hear and harder to accept. Even when others are standing around us, ready to pelt us with stones.

Augustine says in his Sermon 16A.5,

> He was granting pardon, but while he was granting it he raised his face to her and said, "Has no one stoned you?" And she did not say, "Why? What have I done, Lord? I'm not guilty, am I?" That is not what she said. What she said was, "No one, Lord." She accused herself. They had been unable to prove it against her and had withdrawn. But she confessed, because her Lord was not unaware of her guilt but was nonetheless seeking her faith and her confession.[1]

The woman did not try to weasel out of her guilt. She could have blamed the man who was caught with her, but that doesn't appear in the story at all. She could have blamed the Pharisees and experts in the law. She could have blamed circumstances, fears, her husband, the other man's wife. She could have blamed the system, the law, and even Jesus himself.

She did not. She shouldered the blame and only spoke what was true.

In verse ten Jesus asks, "Woman, where are they? Is there no one to condemn you?" These are the first words he speaks to her.

Only Jesus, who chooses not to condemn but to call—to call us to stop sinning and be free—meets the requirements for stone-throwing. And he chooses not to throw but to write in the dirt.

"No one, sir," she replies (v. 11).

No one. Not even the one who has every right. Not even the one who has not sinned, the one who stands before her, the only one left at the scene. He has freed her from being a pawn in the games of others. They are gone.

Now, will he free her from the guilt and shame of her sin?

The Power of Encounter

He does. He says to her, "Neither do I condemn you" (v. 11).

But before he says a word to her, Jesus bends over and writes in the dirt. There has been much speculation about what Jesus may have been writing. Some think he was writing the specific sins of those present. But nobody knows for certain. The original writer of this story didn't think it was necessary to know what he was writing, but did think it was essential that we know he was writing something.

I believe the power of this detail lies not with the content of the writing but in the finger that wrote it.

The English monk Bede (AD 672–735) wrote in his Homilies on the Gospels 1.25, "He desired to write with his finger on the ground, in order to point out that it was he himself who once wrote the Ten Commandments of the law on stone with his finger."[2]

The very finger that wrote the Ten Commandments on stone, now writes in the dirt.

The significance should shake us to the core. He who wrote "You shall not commit adultery" (Exodus 20:14 NIV) indelibly on rock, now writes in sand while rocks are dropped around him and the woman who broke the command.

That is the power of Christ alone. Only he can make the stones fall away.

Jesus does not condemn her, but neither does he dismiss her sin. He forgives her past but he also calls her to righteousness in the future. "Go, and from now on, don't sin anymore," he says (v. 11). The woman is guilty. She knows she's guilty and accepts her guilt. But once guilt has done its job, once it's led to repentance, it's no longer needed.

Jesus tells us, as he tells the woman, to simply go and not sin anymore. Stop sinning. We accept responsibility, shoulder the blame, and then Jesus sets us free with forgiveness and calls us to a new path where guilt for the past has no place. When Jesus frees the woman from condemnation, he also gives her a new start with the words "go and sin no more." Because she encountered Jesus without trying to wiggle out of her guilt, he was able to take it from her and give her freedom in its stead.

He was the only one who could cast a stone. But he chose to bear the weight of her sin himself so that she could begin anew, all because she had an encounter with Jesus at the moment when she wanted nothing more than to hide. All because she stood before him with her sin bared for all to see. Not so for the man who must also have been caught in adultery. He wasn't hauled before Jesus. He seems to have gotten away scot-free. But did he? He doesn't appear at all in the story. He wasn't accused and condemned. He wasn't encircled by rocks in the hands of his enemies. He wasn't publicly humiliated. He wasn't threatened with death. But neither did he encounter Jesus. He wasn't forgiven. He wasn't set free.

Hiding from our sin will never result in our freedom. Because God isn't the God of our hidden sin. God is the God of the first stone.

Who Is This God?

What does it mean that our God is the God of the first stone? It means that only he is qualified to throw stones at all. Religious leaders are not, the crowds are not, fellow sinners and self-proclaimed saints are not. And more importantly, we are not either. Only Jesus, who chooses not to condemn but to call—to call us to stop sinning and be free—meets the requirements for stone-throwing. And he chooses not to throw but to write in the dirt.

It is God's nature to call us not to death but to repentance.

Consider David when he sinned with Bathsheba by not only sleeping with another man's wife but also causing the death of her husband (2 Samuel 11–12). While he hid his sin, there was no freedom, no forgiveness. Sin piled on sin until he was drowning beneath it and others (namely Uriah, Bathsheba's husband) paid the price. But when the prophet Nathan forced David to confront his sin before God, David chose to repent and God restored him. God did not throw the first stone.

Isaiah came to God as a man of unclean lips from a people of unclean lips (Isaiah 6:5). He encountered God and beheld God's glory. God took a glowing coal from around his altar and gave it to one of the winged creatures that were around his throne. The winged creature touched Isaiah's mouth with the coal to take away his guilt and his sin (Isaiah 6:6-7). Isaiah was not condemned but made new. God did not throw a single stone.

Paul pursued Jesus's followers to kill them. But on the road to Damascus, Jesus appeared to Paul in a blinding light (Acts 9). Paul's encounter with Christ caused him to turn from his sin and self-righteousness and he was reborn.

For all, their sin came before God, it wasn't hidden, and God dealt with it without throwing stones. They had an encounter, and it changed everything.

David returned to a life of righteousness and pursuing God. Isaiah became the prophet of God that he was meant to be. Paul became a powerful missionary to the Gentiles.

Our sin does not stop God from fulfilling his purposes for us; only hiding our sin can do that. When we stand before God with no excuses, no one else to blame, and no one else to stop the stones held in the hands of our enemies, only then are we in a position for Jesus to bend down, write in the dirt, and set us free. Only then can we go and sin no more.

> *Lord, when all this pain is my fault, when I'm to blame,*
> *when I've done wrong, made bad choices, made mistakes,*
> *help me to stand before you and not hide from my sin.*
> *Remind me that only you can cast a stone*
> *and only you can make them drop*
> *from the hands of my accusers.*
> *May I trust only, fully, in you as I face my sin*
> *and allow you to free me from my shame.*

When he heard that Jesus of Nazareth was there, he began to shout, "Jesus, Son of David, show me mercy!" Many scolded him, telling him to be quiet, but he shouted even louder, "Son of David, show me mercy!" . . . Throwing his coat to the side, he jumped up and came to Jesus. Jesus asked him, "What do you want me to do for you?" The blind man said, "Teacher, I want to see."

Mark 10:47-48, 50-51

SEE ALSO MARK 10:46-52; MATTHEW 20; LUKE 18.

13

Reaching Through Darkness

I Want to See

Bartimaeus may just be my favorite character in the Bible. There's something about his tenacity, his audacity, and his fierce vivacity that inspires me. He lived in darkness, and yet he saw more clearly than any of his seeing contemporaries. He saw more clearly than I. A blind beggar sitting in the dirt alongside the road to Jerusalem knew what he wanted, and he couldn't be dissuaded from it.

What if I had his vision? What if, in my own darkness, I had his tenacity, audacity, and vivacity? What if all I wanted was to see?

Even as I write these words, I'm filled with a crazy hope, a wild wonder. What *if*, when I am sitting in the dirt, in the dark, in my life, I let none of it stop me from calling out to Jesus? What *if* I don't care what others think but instead cry out all the louder? What *if* I believe that Jesus is who he says he is? What *if* I throw off everything, absolutely everything, that would hinder me, and run in my blindness to him? What *if* I could speak those four simple words, "I want to see"?

Bartimaeus simply does not give two hoots about conforming to what others want. He doesn't care a whit about criticism, rebuke, or reprimands. And so he is free to seek only Jesus.

Lord, give me the heart of Bartimaeus! Give me his courage, his faith, his sight.

For him, it may have happened like this:

A Blind Man Tells His Story

The sun is warm today. Its rays brush my skin, but it brings me no light. The breeze rustles my cloak, and I pull it tighter, leaving the edge free to catch coins if any should come to me. Sometimes I can imagine the way the dust swirls on the road before me. I can almost see the sway of the trees, the clouds that dance across the sky. Sometimes I almost remember the color of wildflowers and the look of laughter on a child's face. Sometimes I remember what it's like to see.

I taste the dust on my lips as I sit alongside the road to Jerusalem. Travelers are coming. I hear their footsteps in the distance. I adjust my cloak for begging. They've left Jericho. They are coming toward me. Many feet, a sizeable crowd.

Today will be a good day. Perhaps several will throw me coins.

The voices approach. Louder, softer, laughter and whispers, all jumbled together. I pick out a few words. Someone is talking about a rich man who walked away. Others mutter about a person named James and his brother, John. A few higher voices, women, I think, whisper something about divorce. They draw closer. And I hear a name. *Jesus.* The voice who spoke the name speaks again. "Ask him what he means when he says the Son of Man will be ridiculed, spit on, killed. How can Jesus be killed?"

Jesus?

Could it be the Jesus from Nazareth, the rabbi, the healer? Could it be the Messiah, the Son of David, who has come to save the lost and heal—a shiver runs through me—and heal the blind?

"Why are we going to Jerusalem with him if he thinks he's going to be killed there?"

"Why do we go anywhere? We follow Jesus the Nazarene!"

It *is* him. He's here. Jesus of Nazareth is among them! I tremble with anticipation and shout out. "Jesus, Son of David, show me mercy!" Can he hear me? Will he stop?

"Quiet, you!" someone hisses.

"Don't bother the teacher."

"Hush." Dirt sprays over me as others keep on scolding me.

"Silence, beggar."

"The rabbi isn't going to throw you any coin."

I don't want money in my cloak. I want so, so much more. I want a miracle.

They continue to rebuke me, but I don't even hear them anymore. Instead I shout all the louder, as loud as I can possibly shout. I shout until the words shake my core and reverberate through the air around me, with all my hope, all my dreams, everything I have ever dared to wish. "Son of David, show me mercy!"

I will not be this close to joy, to wonder, to salvation, and stay silent. I will not be deterred.

The crowd stops. It grows silent. And I hear a voice. A single voice rising from the road before me. "Call him forward."

I almost cry. I almost laugh.

The voices that battered me with their scolding now change their tone. "Be encouraged!" they say. "He's calling you."

He's calling *me*.

I leap to my feet. I kick up dust and throw off my cloak. Coins rattle out of it. I don't care. I leave it behind. I leave it all behind. I don't need it anymore. It is all I own, but it is nothing to me now. Because he is calling me. *He* is calling *me* to him!

"Come!"

I rush toward the voice. I can't see him, but I know he's there. Somewhere. In the darkness, hands grab at me, they push me forward. I focus on his voice and hurry toward it. No darkness can hinder me now. No blindness. No poverty. No fear.

I stop, knowing that he stands before me. I cannot see his face. I cannot see him at all. But I want to. I want to see him.

And then he asks me a single question that penetrates to my very soul. He says, "What do you want me to do for you?"

I don't hesitate. I don't even think twice. "Teacher," I say, "I want to see."

Light and color burst into my vision. And the first thing I see is the face of the one smiling at me. Deep brown eyes look into mine. They crinkle at the edges. And suddenly it is not just my vision that is filled with light. Everything I am is filled with a brilliant joy.

I can see. I see the dust that billows behind him. I see the clouds dancing overhead. I see the yellows and blues of the wildflowers scattered on the hills before me. I see the looks of awe and wonder on the faces of those around me. I see it all. And yet all that matters is that I see him.

I laugh.

He laughs with me. "Go, your faith has healed you."

Go? I will go. I will go wherever he leads. I will follow him to Jerusalem, I will follow him to his death. When he's spit on, ridiculed, killed, I will follow.

I will follow him because now I truly see.

Reaching for Wonder

Jesus's encounter with Bartimaeus is the last such healing and disciple-making that we will see before Jesus is arrested and killed in Jerusalem. Jesus and his disciples are traveling with a crowd on the road from Jericho to Jerusalem. He has just told his followers that he "didn't come to be served but rather to serve and to give his life to liberate many people" (Mark 10:45). A few verses prior he explained his death and resurrection to the twelve, who didn't understand him. He spoke of how he would be handed over to the chief priests and the experts in the law. He told them that he would be condemned to death, handed over to the Gentiles. He would be ridiculed, spat on, tortured, and killed. After three days, he would rise up. All this hangs in the air as Jesus leaves Jericho on the final stage of the journey to Jerusalem.

Soon, people will travel the fifteen miles from Jericho to Jerusalem with palm branches for Jesus's triumphal entry into Jerusalem. Soon, he will be arrested. Soon condemned. Soon crucified.

On that road to death sits Bartimaeus, a blind beggar who still dares to hope. He will be the last one to ask for healing. He will be the last one to become a follower of Jesus before Jesus is hung on a Roman cross.

The last one who finally, after all this time, gets it right.

Shout All the Louder

As soon as Bartimaeus hears that Jesus is among the crowd walking by him, he shouts out. He hopes, he reaches, he dares to call for the one thing he believes this Son of David can give: Mercy. He asks for something he doesn't deserve, but knows he needs. "Jesus, Son of David, show me mercy!" (v. 47).

Everyone around him rebukes him for it. They know he doesn't deserve it either. He is a blind beggar sitting along the roadside. They tell him to be quiet, to be invisible, to disappear.

So when you're afraid you've missed him. When you're sitting in your darkness and blindness, terrorized by the fear that God has come and gone and you didn't recognize him, take heart! Be encouraged! He's calling to you.

But this man, sitting in his world of darkness, believes more strongly in Jesus and who Jesus is than he worries about what others think of him. He doesn't care about that at all.

In fact, in the face of discouragement, he cries out all the louder and all the more: "Son of David, show me mercy!" (v. 48).

I am reminded of the parable of the persistent widow in Luke 18, and of Jacob, who wrestled with an angel all night and wouldn't let go until he was blessed (Genesis 32). That kind of fierce faith inspires me because it cannot be quenched by the discouragement of others. Bartimaeus simply does not give two hoots about conforming to what others want. He doesn't care a whit about criticism, rebuke, or reprimands. And so he is free to seek only Jesus.

To not care what others think. To be focused only on Christ. To see, though blind and in darkness, Jesus for who he really is. To call him David's son . . .

Bartimaeus is the only one in the book of Mark to call Jesus the "Son of David." That term is heavy with significance. The Son of David, another term for Israel's Messiah, would bring about all the promises and the redemption of Israel. Using the term "Son of David" was meant to recall God's favor during Israel's golden age and all the promises made to David that he would always have a descendant on the throne. It was also meant to recall the words of Isaiah, who promised that this Messiah would be given as:

> A covenant to the people,
> as a light to the nations,
> to open blind eyes, to lead the prisoners from
> prison,
> and those who sit in darkness from the dungeon.
> —Isaiah 42:6b-7

To Bartimaeus, Jesus is not just a wandering rabbi. He's not just a healer or a teacher. He is this one who was promised to open the eyes of the blind and free those sitting in darkness. He is the promise of God to his people. He is the promise of God to Bartimaeus. And Bartimaeus dares to believe it, to believe all of it.

Here there is no "if you want" or "if you are able." No, Bartimaeus goes all in. He holds nothing back. He stakes everything on the belief that this Jesus of Nazareth is the Son of David who will fulfill all God has said, and will fulfill it for him.

That is an audacious faith.

Be Encouraged! He's Calling You.

And then the voices change. Instead of "sit down and shut up," they start saying, "Take heart! Be encouraged! Buck up! He's calling you."

In your darkness, in your blindness, Jesus is calling you. *He is calling you.* And he's calling you in a way that you can hear. He doesn't motion to the blind man. He calls to him. He uses a sense that Bartimaeus can receive.

He leaves behind everything he once counted on when he comes to Jesus. He comes to Jesus with nothing but his need. Nothing. Not his good name, not his good deeds, not his good thoughts. Nothing but his need and his faith. His tenacious, audacious faith.

So when you're afraid you've missed him. When you're sitting in your darkness and blindness, terrorized by the fear that God has come and gone and you didn't recognize him, take heart! Be encouraged! He's calling to you. He's calling to you in a way in which you can hear. And you can do as Bartimaeus did—you can jump up and run to him.

Of all the Gospel accounts, Mark is the only one that includes the detail of how Bartimaeus flung off his coat. (Mark is also the only one to include Bartimaeus's name.) What a powerful image! As a blind beggar, Bartimaeus most likely had only one possession—his cloak. He used it to keep warm, to keep off the sun, probably to sleep, and perhaps most importantly, to catch the coins that people would toss to him. He wouldn't be able to see coins that fell around him, but he could feel them as they plunked on his coat. Everything he had, everything he depended on, was embodied in that cloak. And blind Bartimaeus just tosses it aside.

Nothing else that we are asking for, hoping for, praying for, matters so much as seeing him.

He leaves behind everything he once counted on when he comes to Jesus. He comes to Jesus with nothing but his need. Nothing. Not his good name, not his good deeds, not his good thoughts. Nothing but his need and his faith. His tenacious, audacious faith.

What Do You Want?

And Jesus asks him one simple question: "What do you want me to do for you?" (v. 51). A few verses prior, Jesus had just asked this question of James and John, two of his closest disciples. They answered by telling him they wanted to sit at his right and left hand in glory. They wanted position. They wanted prestige.

But what Bartimaeus wants is the very thing God longs to give. Bartimaeus wants mercy, and mercy is sight.

In one of the most beautiful, simplistic answers in the Bible, Bartimaeus says, "Teacher, I want to see" (v. 51).

I want to see.

For every person sitting in his or her own personal darkness, or every one of us who feels blind and cut off, for all of us who are sitting in the dirt beside the road to Jerusalem, those four simple words should be our prayer.

I want to see.

I want to see Jesus.

Nothing else that we are asking for, hoping for, praying for, matters so much as seeing him. Seeing him on the road, seeing him on his way to the place where he will die and rise again, seeing him as he looks into our face and tells us, "Go!"

And like Bartimaeus, once we see him, once we really see him, we will follow him anywhere, even to the cross.

Who Is This God?

Who is this God of Sight who is calling us out of our darkness so that we may see the face of God?

He is the God of Moses, who asked of him, "Please show me your glorious presence" (Exodus 33:18). And God placed Moses in the cleft of the rock so he could glimpse the glory of God. Moses, like Bartimaeus, asked God to make him see. And his sight changed everything.

He is the God of Isaiah, who in the year that King Uzziah died, saw the Lord, high and lifted up on his exalted throne. His robe filled the temple, and winged creatures shouted, "Holy, holy, holy is the Lord of heavenly forces! All the earth is filled with God's glory!" And the Lord said, "Whom should I send, and who will go for us?" Isaiah said, "I'm here; send me" (Isaiah 6:3, 8). And God said, just as he said to Bartimaeus, "Go."

He is the God of Peter, James, and John, who went with Jesus to the top of a very high mountain where they saw Jesus transformed before them. His clothes were amazingly bright, and Elijah and Moses appeared with him. They saw Jesus, for a moment, for who he really is.

When we see Jesus for who he actually is, when we encounter him in his glory, everything changes. We change. Because darkness has always been just a precursor to incredible light.

When we see Jesus for who he actually is, when we encounter him in his glory, everything changes. We change. Because darkness has always been just a precursor to incredible light.

We know this because when Jesus hung on the cross, dying, darkness came over the land for three hours in the middle of the day. Everyone lived in eerie blackness from noon to three o'clock. And in that darkness, the curtain in the temple was torn in two from top to bottom. The curtain that separated us from seeing the Holy of Holies was forever broken. The darkness gave way to sight.

So when you're kneeling in the dark at the foot of the cross, when you can't see your way forward, can't see your way back, when all you can hear is the dripping of death and the groans of the dying, remember, the curtain is being torn away. You will see God.

And in the darkness of the tomb before the break of dawn, when Jesus seems hidden, when it seems all is lost and dead and gone, remember, it is almost the third day. Soon, the stone will be rolled away, the angels will come, and the tomb will be flooded with incredible light. You will see the risen Lord.

And in the darkness alongside the road, when everyone is telling you to just shut up and give up, remember, Jesus is calling you. He is calling you to come boldly to him. You will see the face of God.

Sometimes we just need to wait in hope for the sky to clear, for the stone to be rolled away, for the crowd to stop long enough for us to hear his voice. Sometimes we are blind, but God will restore our sight. Sometimes we can hear nothing but death and despair, but God is about to rise again. It is what God does; it is who he is.

And when we see him, when he truly restores our sight so we can see him for who he truly is . . . that is the answer, that is the remedy for all our pain, all our struggles, every hard thing we must endure. And that is the purpose for every struggle. That we may cry out, "Jesus, Son of David, have mercy. . . ." That darkness may be broken and we may truly see.

Lord, I want to see . . .

When they came to Emmaus . . . they urged him, saying,
"Stay with us. It's nearly evening, and the day is almost
over. . . . He took the bread, blessed and broke it, and
gave it to them. Their eyes were opened and they recog-
nized him, but he disappeared from their sight. They
said to each other, "Weren't our hearts on fire when he
spoke to us along the road and when he explained the
scriptures for us?"

Luke 24:28-32

SEE ALSO LUKE 24:13-34.

14

REACHING FOR WONDER

Hearts on Fire

A nd so we come to the final encounter on our journey. We've met Jesus along the roadside, at the temple, along the Sea of Galilee, in the crowds, and at the edge of a well. We've seen him heal the blind, raise up the dead and paralyzed, and free those bound by shame, pain, and doubt. We've watched him soothe and scold, break bonds and beckon us near. We've peeked at his encounters with hurting people who were at the low points in their lives. And we've imagined what it would be like for him to encounter us in those same ways.

Now we come to the last encounter. Two men walk from Jerusalem toward the village of Emmaus, seven miles away. They carry with them dark disappointment, deep doubt, and the emptiness of dreams that they believe can never come true. They had believed. They had hoped. They had dreamed of freedom for themselves and for Israel.

And then Jesus died on a Roman cross.

Can you even imagine . . .

Imagine . . .

Imagine that everything you've ever hoped for is gone. Imagine that your dreams for the future have been stolen and crushed. There is nothing you can do to make it better. There is no song you can sing, no prayer you can pray, no hope you can cling to.

It is all dead. Gone.

In his death and resurrection, we see the truth. Nothing dead cannot be raised. Nothing hurt cannot be healed. Nothing lost cannot be found. Even us. Even our hopes. Even our dreams. Even the God who we thought had failed us.

And you are leaving it all behind you as you simply walk away.

You've been told there's reason to hope. There are rumors, there are stories. But you don't hope. Not anymore.

Imagine that you've read through an entire book that beckons you to believe again, to trust again, to look for a God you saw die. And now you are reading the last chapter and the pain remains, no healing has come, no change at all in the circumstances that surround you.

And you are ready to close the book and simply walk away.

You head down the road, you argue with a friend. You discuss why hope is foolish and life simply is what it is and nothing will ever change.

But a third man joins you. You don't recognize him at all. He asks you what you're talking about and you shake your head. How could he not know, how could he not see?

So you explain your hope and what became of it. You lay out your dreams and how they died. You fight the tears because you've already cried too much, struggled too much, hurt too much.

You fling your story in his face, daring him to deny your pain, your hopelessness, the deadness of your despair. You tell him again. It is all dead. Gone. Done.

But then something unexpected happens. The stranger begins to explain everything to you, not just the circumstances that caused your pain. He goes back to the beginning. He shows you how it all fits together. How every single thing in your life comes together for good because you love God and you—you!—are called according to his purposes. It all makes sense. Nothing that has happened, no pain, no suffering, no disappointment, no failure, no death is left purposeless. It is all woven together like a beautiful tapestry, with dark threads and light.

So you ask the stranger to stay with you as the day turns to night.

Imagine sitting with him at the table. He lifts his arms. He breaks the bread. And only then do you recognize this stranger from the road. It is Jesus, who died for you, rose for you, and has come to encounter you when all you wanted to do was get away.

You recognize him in the breaking of the bread.

And you realize that your heart is on fire within you.

Suddenly, you dare to hope again. And you turn right back around and head the way you came. You trudged on your way out but you run on your way back.

You run back to hope, back to joy, back to faith.

All because Jesus met you when you were running away.

All because you encountered him on the road to Emmaus.

Reaching for Wonder

When all is lost, when rumors of hope fall on deaf ears, when dreams are dead and you're walking away, remember: Jesus walks with you. You may not recognize him. You might think he abandoned you back in Jerusalem. You may think he's dead.

But he is there, walking next to you.

Someday he will even explain it all. You will understand why the pain came, why struggles were necessary. Keep listening, keep walking, and dare to break bread with him.

We recognize him in the breaking of the bread, in communion. "This is my body, which is given for you," he says (Luke 22:19). In his death and resurrection, we see the truth. Nothing dead cannot be raised. Nothing hurt cannot be healed. Nothing lost cannot be found. Even us. Even our hopes. Even our dreams. Even the God who we thought had failed us.

On the road to Emmaus, we will encounter him. We will see him. We will finally see . . . and our hearts will be set ablaze with wonder.

Who Are You?

In your pain, in your suffering and toil, are you willing to walk on the road with him? Will you listen for his voice? Will you invite him to the table to break bread? Will you allow him to reach through your discouragement and disillusionment and reveal to you the wonder of who he really is, the wonder of your life with him?

If you do, more than healing, more than freedom, more than you ever dreamed will be yours. Your heart will be set on fire with the wonder of his love for you.

Do you dare reach for wonder?

> *Lord, walk with me and help me to see.*
> *Set my heart on fire for you.*
> *May I always, forever reach for your wonder.*

Note to the Reader

Dear Fellow Christ-Encounterer,

Thank you for walking with me through these one-time encounters with Christ in the New Testament.

As I wrote this book, I was living through one of the hardest years of my life. We had sickness and scares, threats to my family, and times, so many times, when I didn't know what to do or how to move forward out of the horror. And every chapter I wrote became a lifeline for me personally. I wept as I wrote, and I tried to hear what God was telling me. The stories, the truths, in *Reaching for Wonder* helped me through. They helped me to see God and to persevere and to dare to hope.

I pray they did the same for you. And I pray that when your life hurts, you will walk with him, hear his words, and not turn away. I pray you will say, "Lord, I want to see . . ." and that you will dare to break bread with him. I pray you will be healed of your fear, your shame, your blindness, deafness, or muteness, and you will be able to walk again, to walk with him again in joy and hope and indescribable wonder.

Reaching for Wonder,
Marlo

A NOTE TO THE READER

If you'd like to know more about me or my other books, please visit my website at VividGod.com and sign up for my newsletter, or join me for thoughts on finding the wonder of God in everyday life on Twitter (www.twitter.com/MarloSchalesky) or Facebook (www .facebook.com/MarloSchalesky). I hope to hear from you!

Acknowledgments

In some ways, this book was the easiest I've ever written because each chapter poured from my soul. In other ways, it was most difficult because every word had to be pulled from a bleeding heart. So, I want to thank my husband, Bryan, for his steadfast support of me through the process. He believed in this book from the beginning and stood by me when I struggled to put words to paper (or computer screen!) and faithfully read every chapter as I finished each one.

Thanks too to my kids for (mostly) letting me write when I needed to write. Thanks for cooking dinners and cleaning up (mostly) when I needed to delve deeper in the evening hours. And thanks for walking with your dad and me through this year of troubles and triumphs and remaining faithful to the God who calls us to follow him.

And finally, thanks to the young adult group at Salinas Valley Community Church, who talked me through the early stories so we could see what we could see and find the wonder hidden in each story of an encounter with the living God.

I appreciate you all so much!

NOTES

2. Reaching Through Shame

1. Bruce Milne, *The Message of John*, The Bible Speaks Today (Leicester, England: InterVarsity, 1993), 83.

2. D. A. Carson, *The Gospel According to John*, The Pillar New Testament Commentary (Grand Rapids, MI: Eerdmans, 1991), 228.

3. Michael Card, *Parable of Joy: Reflections on the Wisdom of the Book of John* (Nashville: Thomas Nelson, 1995), 57.

4. Paul Louis Metzger, *The Gospel of John: When Love Comes to Town* (Downers Grove, IL: IVP Books, 2010), 77.

3. Reaching Through Helplessness

1. Michael Card, *Mark: The Gospel of Passion* (Downers Grove, IL: IVP Books, 2012), 46.

2. Arthur A. Just Jr., ed., *Ancient Christian Commentary on Scripture: New Testament III: Luke* (Downers Grove, IL: InterVarsity, 2003), 92.

4. Reaching Through Loss

1. Michael Card, *Luke: The Gospel of Amazement* (Downers Grove, IL: IVP Books, 2011), 98.

2. David E. Garland, *Luke*, Zondervan Exegetical Commentary on the New Testament (Grand Rapids, MI: Zondervan, 2011), 301.

5. Reaching Through the Voices Within

1. David E. Garland, *Luke*, Zondervan Exegetical Commentary on the New Testament (Grand Rapids, MI: Zondervan, 2011), 357.

2. Garland, *Luke*, 359.

6. Reaching Through Desperation

1. Michael Card, *Luke: The Gospel of Amazement* (Downers Grove, IL: IVP Books, 2011), 116.

7. Reaching Through Despair

1. David E. Garland, *Luke*, Zondervan Exegetical Commentary on the New Testament (Grand Rapids, MI: Zondervan, 2011), 369.
2. Garland, *Luke*, 369.

8. Reaching Through Excuses

1. Michael Card, *Parable of Joy: Reflections on the Wisdom of the Book of John* (Nashville: Thomas Nelson, 1995), 65.
2. Card, *Parable of Joy*, 65–66.
3. Craig Sheaffer, *Introduction to Agronomy*, 2nd ed., Just the Facts101 (Moore Park, CA: Content Technologies, 2014).

10. Reaching Through Isolation

1. Thomas C. Oden & Christopher A. Hall, ed., *Ancient Christian Commentary on Scripture: New Testament II: Mark* (Downers Grove, IL: IVP Academic, 1998), 104.
2. Michael Card, *Mark: The Gospel of Passion* (Downers Grove, IL: IVP Books, 2012), 102.

12. Reaching Through Guilt

1. Joel C. Elowsky, ed., *Ancient Christian Commentary on Scripture: New Testament IVa: John 1–10* (Downers Grove, IL: IVP Academic, 2006), 277.
2. Elowsky, *Ancient Christian Commentary IVa*, 274.

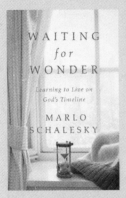